GW01149136

الى قمري الجميل

خليل ٢٢/١٢/١٩٩٤م

Feathers and the horizon

feathers
and the horizon

A selection of modern poetry from across the Arab world.

Anne Fairbairn • Ghazi al-Gosaibi

With a Foreword by A.D.Hope

THE LEROS PRESS 1989

THE LEROS PRESS 1989
The Leros Press, Canberra
Australian Capital Territory 1989

This book is copyright. Apart from any fair dealing for the purposes of private study, research, criticism, or review, as permitted under the Copyright Act, no part may be reproduced by any process without written permission.
Enquiries should be made to the publishers: The Leros Press, PO Box 18, Duffy, ACT 2611, Australia.

ISBN 0 949264 56 3

Australia Council | Arts for Australians

Publication assisted by the Literature Board of the Australia Council, the Federal Government's arts and funding advisory body; and by the Australian Department of Foreign Affairs and Trade.

SECOND EDITION, NOVEMBER 1989

To those who bring light upon light

Foreword

The Poetry of the Arabs

THE VAST EXTENT of the peoples who make up the Arab-speaking world today is marked perhaps more by its differences and its divisions than by its cohesion and any principle of similarity. But two things bind it together: its religion and its poetry.

Indeed, the two may be said to have begun in double harness, for in the central and most sacred spot in Mecca itself, we learn that there are preserved the seven famous odes, the Mu'allaquat, a word that has been variously translated as 'the golden ones', 'the choice or exquisite' and 'the suspended ones'. These are reputed to be the finest flower of Arabian poetry before the coming of Islam in the sixth century.

Be that as it may, when I was asked to comment briefly on the present volume, I had to admit that my small acquaintance with Arabic was confined to the classical period and that I was quite unable to make any assessment of the various aspects that distinguish it today. All I can say is that it seems to me a miraculous achievement for Anne Fairbairn, Ghazi al-Gosaibi, to have brought and held together poets from so many countries who are working in so many new directions.

This has not been achieved without many journeys and immense labour on the part of Anne herself, and she well deserves the great honour conferred on her in the form of the Annual Gibran International Award. That Award marks a literary achievement of the first order, the publication of a work of a kind never seen before in which an Australian poet interprets for fellow-Australians the works of Arab poets writing in their own language.

But it is not only a literary event. It has a political and social importance which we cannot yet foresee and which certainly will help to break down those barriers which so sadly divide us today.

A.D.Hope
AO OBE EMERITUS PROFESSOR

Acknowledgments

ANNE FAIRBAIRN AND THE LEROS PRESS wish to thank the following people and institutions for their support, advice and encouragement.

Darwish Mustapha Alfa, Ali and Salma Alireza, HE Tariq Almoayed, HE Abdul Rahman Alohaly, Nassan Amiri (who has handwritten all the calligraphy), Gay Andrews, Samar Attar, Australia-Arab Heritage League, Lewis Awad, Kareem Barbara and all members of his family, Michael Body, Sarah Body, Adam Body, Issa Boullata, Des Cahill, Annabel Davie, Alan Deacon, Department of Foreign Affairs and Trade, Sir Robert and Lady Drew, M.A.El Erian and his wife, Wahia, Rida al-Feeli, Shadia Gedeon, Monkeith Kachish al-Geita, James Gordon, Bruce Grant, Jud al-Haj, A.D. Hope (for constant encouragement and faith in my concept of poetic action), HE Latif Abul-Husn, the Government of Iraq, Iraqi Airways, Jabra Ibrahim Jabra, Amal Jaffa, HE Latif Nusayyif Jassim, Ahmed Jusef, Hussam al-Khatibe, Kraft Foods Ltd, Literature Board of the Australia Council, Abdel Wahid Lulua, Meadow Lea Foods Ltd, Maurice Mubarack (for generously allowing access to his Sydney office), Abd al-Aziz al-Maqalih, Kamel Murr, Fuad Namour, the National Library, Canberra, the Philip Institute, Melbourne, Poets at Mirbed in Baghdad, Sigrid al-Qusaibi and her children Yara, Suhail, Faris and Nijad (Professor Links), Judith Rodriguez, HE Abdul Aziz Rowas, Abdullah M. Sadiq, Nurradin Sammud, Ali Shalash, Tom Shapcott, Ahmed Suleiman, Douglas Sturkey, Anna and Evan Thomas, Ustaad Ibrahim al-Urrayad, Evan Williams, Adrian Young and the ANU Graphic Design studio.

Anne Fairbairn would particularly like to thank HRH Prince Abdullah al-Faysal al-Saud, whose dedication to Arabic poetry has been a constant source of inspiration to her; for his sake and for the sake of all poets of the Arab world, she hopes that *Feathers and the Horizon* will help to keep alive their great literary heritage in far-flung Australia.

Every attempt has been made to obtain the personal permission of each of the poets represented here for the reproduction and translation of their work. Whenever it was possible to make contact with the poets concerned, permission was gladly and freely given, and for this the translators and publishers wish to express their thanks.

Apologies are offered to any who could not be contacted: they are invited to write to the publishers so that amends may be made in any subsequent editions. We thank Ahmed Shboul and Tony Maron for their most helpful critical amendments for the second edition.

Anne Fairbairn and the Leros Press wish to thank the Blue Star Line for shipping bulk orders of *Feathers and the Horizon* freight-free to the Middle East.

Contents

Foreword

Acknowledgments

Introduction

A note on the translation

Poets and poems

The order in which the poems appear is according to the alphabetical order of the family names of the poets.

LUTFI LA'FAR AMAN • *Fawzia* 18

LAME'A ABBAS AMARAH • *Image* 20

HILAL AL-AMIRI • *Knight in Armour* 22

SAI'D AQL • *You a Yacht and To Sail* 24

HASAN FATH AL-BAB • *Homework* 26

SHAWQI BAGHDADI • *Friendship* 30

HAMRI BAHRI • *The Butterfly* 32

ABDULLAH AL-BARADUNI • *Her Hands* 34

ABD AL-WAHAB AL-BAYATI • *The Face and the Mirror* 36

BABHA BIN BEDAYWAH • *Facing Death* 38

MAHMUD DARWISH • *Defiance* 40

AMAL DUNQAL • *Against Whom?* 42

MUHAMMAD HASAN FAQI • *West and East* 44

MUHAMMAD AL-FAYIZ • *Tune 69* 46

ABDULLAH AL-FAYSAL • *Daughter of Sadness* 48

MUHAMMAD AL-FAYTURI • *The Moon and the Garden* 50

MUHAMMAD ABDUH GHANIM • *In the Carriage* 52

MUHAMMAD AL-GHAZZI • *Your Eyes Will Not Perceive* 54

QASIM HADDAD • *The Pearl* 56

BULAND AL-HAIDARI • *A Premature Elegy* 58

SARAH HARIB (pen name) • *I Turned Towards You and Prayed* 62

MUHAMMAD AL-HARITHI • *Beloved I've Been Here Since Morning* 64

ZAFIR AL-HASAN • *I Want to Be* 68

KHALIL HAWI • *The Miracle* 70

AHMAD ABD AL-MU'TI HIJAZI • *The City .. and I* 72

MUHAMMAD AL-MAKKI IBRAHIM • *Elegy* 74

SAMA' ISA • *Cradle* 76

BADAWI AL-JABBAL • *The Crushed Doll* 78

MUHAMMAD MAHDI AL-JAWAHIRI • *Transplant of Conscience* 80

SALMA AL-KHADRA AL-JAYYUSI • *Awakening* 82

ILYAS KHALIL JURYIS • *Apology to God* 84

YUSUF AL-KHAL • *Death* 88

BISHARAH AL-KHURI (AL-AKHTAL AL-SAGHIR) • *Twice* 90

SALAH LABAKI • *The Storm* 92

HASAN AL-LAWZI • *Her Face and the Wall* 94

ILIYA ABU MADI • *Neither You Nor I* 96

HAYDAR MAHMUD • *From the Rubayi't of Sinbad* 98

ALI MIRZA MAHMUD • *I Love You .. How Should I Love You?* 100

AHMAD AL-MAJATI • *Fear* 102

JA'FAR MAJID • *Silence* 104

NAZIK AL-MALA'IKAH • *Elegy for a Woman of No Consequence* 106

SHAFIQ AL-MA'LUF • *The Peasant* 108

ABD AL-AZIZ AL-MAQALIH • *A Song for Ashes* 110
AHMAD MATAR • *A Pen* 112
AHMAD AL-SAFI AL-NAJAFI • *Garments of the Soul* 114
IBRAHIM NAJI • *Burning Letters* 116
IBRAHIM NASRALLAH • *Windows* 118
ISA AL-NA'URI • *In Hospital* 120
NIZAR QABBANI • *Her Daughter* 122
SAMIH AL-QASIM • *Suitcase* 124
HASAN ABDULLAH AL-QURASHI • *To Whom the Glory?* 126
GHAZI AL-QUSAIBI (AL-GOSAIBI) • *Oh Desert* 128
ABD AL-RAHMAN RAFI' • *Palm Tree* 132
GEELI ABD AL-RAHMAN • *Perplexity* 134
ABD AL-MUN'IM AL-RIFA'I • *To My Son Omar* 136
UMAR ABU RISHAH • *Read Them - Papers of a Dead Man* 138
ADIB SA'B • *Clouds Without Rain* 140
ALI AL-SAB'TI • *City of Human Beings* 142
SALAH ABD AL-SABUR • *Eulogy for an Insignificant Man* 146
ALI AHMAD SA'ID (ADONIS) • *I Told You* 148
MUHAMMAD AL-AKHDAR AL-SA'IHI • *Feminine and Masculine* 150
AHMAD SALIH AL-SALIH • *Perhaps* 152
RU'A SALIM (pen name) • *To the Fathomless Depths Take Me* 154
NURRADIN SAMMUD • *Her Birthday* 156
MUHAMMAD AL-SARGHINI • *If the City Wished* 158
GEORGE SAYDAH • *In the Garden* 162
HABIB AL-SAYEGH • *The Vacation* 164

YUSUF AL-SAYEGH • *Sound* 166
BADR SHAKIR AL-SAYYAB • *Burning* 168
ILYAS ABU SHABAKAH • *The Cup* 170
AHMAD AL-SHARIF • *The Poet's House* 172
ALI AL-SHARQAWI • *Rain* 174
MUHAMMAD IBRAHIM ABU SINNAH • *The Sad Star* 178
HUSAIN SIRHAN • *Moznah* 180
ABD AL-KARIM AL-TABBAL • *Shells* 182
MUBARAK BIN SAIF AL THANI • *The Remains of a Pearling Dhow* 184
FADWA TUQAN • *Existence* 188
AZRAJ UMAR • *Love Songs* 190
IBRAHIM AL-USTA UMAR • *The Answer* 192
MUHAMMAD UMRAN • *A Dream or a Bet?* 194
IBRAHIM AL-URAYYID • *The Child in Me* 196
THURAYYA AL-URAYYID • *The Night* 198
MAHMUD ABU AL'WAFA • *A Sacred Day* 200
AL-MUNSIF AL-WAHAYBI • *The Desert* 202
ABD AL-RAZAQ ABD AL-WAHID • *Drop of Sadness* 204
KHALIFA AL-WUQAYYAN • *Sailing with the Wind* 206
ISA AL-YASIRI • *Tonight We Wake You With Roses* 208
SA'DI YUSUF • *Grief* 210
MUHAMMAD MAHMUD AL-ZUBAIRI • *Moments of Inspiration* 212
Biographical notes on the poets 214
Transliteration of poets' names 221
Other publications of the Leros Press 224

Introduction

IN 1986 WHEN I WAS INVITED by The Leros Press to compile a volume of Arabic poetry with parallel text in English, I accepted with enthusiasm, even though I was aware I was ill-equipped for the task. My encounter with the Arab world has been so enriching I wanted an opportunity to share my experience with fellow Australians. What better way than through poetry?

My serious interest in Arabic literature began in 1980 when, on a flight to London during a particularly distressing period in my life, I decided to break my journey in Syria. At a dinner party in Damascus, I was introduced to Dr Hussam al-Khatibe, who teaches Arabic studies at the university. He told me that Arabs are passionate about their language and are by nature poets. He explained that classical Arabic poetry is still being written, using the same forms, metre, images, rhymes and themes used by poets more than a thousand years ago, but that many 20th century poets are struggling to find new poetic forms to express more adequately how they feel about the immense changes taking place about them.

The Australian and American guests sat in rapt silence as he recited poems by Syrian poet Adonis (Ali Ahmad Said), a leader of the free verse movement, Palestinian poet Fadwa Tuqan, and a classical poem by Yemeni poet Muhammad Mahmoud al-Zubairi. I realised that the unique literary heritage of the Arab world and the exciting 'new' poetry being written this century are unknown to most Australians. I made up my mind to try to build a bridge of poems between Australia and the Arab world. The construction of this bridge has involved considerable effort and determination and several years of my life, but has proved to be miraculously spiritually healing, both through encounter and hard work. I have come to regard my first visit to Damascus and all that has flowed from it as my personal 'Road to Damascus'.

Dr Hussam was enthusiastic about my bridge of poems, so in 1982 I returned to Syria taking books on behalf of the Australia Council's Literature Board to help build his end of our bridge - a volume of Australian literature. As editor of *Al-Adab Al-Ajnabiyya*, a quarterly on world literature, Dr Hussam planned his volume to appear as a special issue containing translations into Arabic of Australian poetry, fiction and drama.

While I was a guest of the University of San'aa in Yemen in 1985, Dr Hani Raheb, a Syrian writer and academic, offered to translate a number of Australian poems into Arabic for Dr Hussam's special issue. In 1987 Dr Hussam visited Australia, bringing with him the completed volume. On the cover was a drawing of a kangaroo with Australian books spilling from its pouch. One end of our bridge of poems had been built.

In 1986 I visited Saudi Arabia and Bahrain in search of poetry from the Arabian Gulf region to include in the Leros Press volume. Dr Ghazi al-Gosaibi, Saudi Arabian ambassador to Bahrain and a leading modern poet, offered to help. I accepted his offer and we discussed how we would tackle the work. We decided to select poems from every Arab country in order to symbolise the essential unity of spirit among the people of the Arab nation; to include poems written during the last 50 years from all major 20th century schools including the Classical School, since even in this climate of change classical poets have no plans to fold their tents and silently drift away; also to include poems from the 'grey' overlapping areas, which make up a multiplicity of minor schools between the clearly defined work of major schools, but to exclude prose poems. To choose poems with themes common to all humanity such as poverty, death, love parenthood; themes that transcend racial, religious and political differences; and to include poetry by lesser known as well as better known poets. Above all we decided to treat this selection as an introduction for newcomers to the subject.

However, the volume's strength may prove to be its weakness: our desire to introduce readers to poetry from all Arab countries and to represent all major schools has made it impossible to do justice to each country or each school.

For the reader to understand the background of the poems we have selected, I shall outline briefly the changing face of Arabic poetry in the 20th century, mentioning poets whose work we have included.

Towards the end of Ottoman rule, by returning for inspiration to the purity and freshness of the work of the early masters of classical poetry, the Egyptian poet Mahmoud Sami al-Barudi (1839-1904) and his followers made a determined effort to revitalise the stagnant, stilted poetry of the day. Their work is now considered to belong to the Neo-Classical School. Ironically, since these poets were looking far back into the past for renewal, their initiative heralded radical change. However, many poets such as (Iraqi) Muhammad Mahdi al-Jawahiri continued to write in a Neo-Classical style later this century.

Gradually, as a result of expanding contact with the West, a growing sense of the significance of the individual and concern for cultural and social change emerged and poets restlessly experimented with new forms of expression. This tendency was reinforced by the poets of the Mahjar School. (Poets who migrated to the Americas from Lebanon, Syria and Palestine were known as Mahjar poets.) These poets, exposed to western vitality and materialism, yet nostalgic for their cultural and spiritual heritage, began writing with a new voice. The most influential of these was (Lebanese) Gibran Khalil Gibran (1883-1931) who founded a literary society, al-Rabitah al-Qalamiyah (The Pen League) in New York in 1920.

The Pre-Romantic School was established early in this century by Khalil Mutran (1872-1949), a Lebanese-born Egyptian poet who revolutionised Arabic society by insisting on a new organic unity of meaning within poems. This was a radical change from the traditional emphasis on meaning being encapsulated in individual lines, with a poem being made up of a number of such lines. Influenced by the French Romantics, Mutran was concerned with subjective, more lyrical writing as seen in the poetry of (Lebanese) Bishara al-Khuri.

Three Egyptian poets, Abdul Rahman Shukri, Abdul Qader al-Mazini and Abbass Mahmoud al-Aqqad were young contemporaries of Mutran. Influenced by him and the English Romantics and opposed to the Neo-Classical School, they formed the Diwan Group which stands out as having put a new emphasis on emotional content and the use of simpler language.

The Romantic School emerged between the two world wars as a rather belated response to British Romantic poetry. The influence of the Diwan Group, the Mahjar poets and the Cairo literary magazine Apollo (founded by Dr Abu Shadi) helped spread the popularity of Romantic poetry. Egyptian Romantic poet Dr Ibrahim Naji was a friend and collaborator of Abu Shadi. Romantic poetry profoundly influenced the Syrian poet Umar Abu Risha and (Lebanese) Illyas Abu Shabakah (also deeply influenced by Baudelaire) both of whom became Romantic 'greats'.

After World War II, poets of the Romantic School, accused of escapism, especially in view of the appalling postwar poverty and the events that unfolded in Palestine, felt compelled to face issues of degradation and suffering. Many intellectuals and poets turned to Marxism to try to help solve their problems of conscience. Political points were made in an imagery enriched by a new use of collective mythology, but expression was kept subjective and the language simple, as a result of the Romantic experience. This new wave of poets came to be known as Social Realists and few poets escaped their influence. Iraqi poets Abd al-Wahhab al-Bayati and Balund al-Haydari, the Egyptian poet, Salah Abd al-Sabur and Sudanese poet, Muhammad al-Fayturi all clearly demonstrate a new social conscience in their work. Even the Syrian Romantic Nizar Qabbani joined their ranks.

Encounter with modern British poetry in the middle of this century, especially the work of T.S. Eliot, had a profound effect on Arabic poetry, both technically, with greater freedom in form and metre, and in content. Poets began to express feelings of loss, alienation and despair as they observed how the abundant West, by championing the tyranny of money, creates an inner 'wasteland'. These feelings were compounded by the gradual erosion of traditional values in the Arab world. Eliot's influence is clear in the work of Salah Abd al-Sabur and (Lebanese) Khalil Hawi.

In the late 1940s and '50s many poets felt compelled to move further away from limiting rhyme and metre in order to speak with a symbolically 'freer' voice. Lewis Awad (1915-) is an Egyptian academic and literary critic; his Kiriyalayson is one of the earliest experiments in Arabic free verse. Iraqi poets Nazik al-Malai'ka and Badr Shakir al-Sayyab demonstrated, in poems published in 1947, a clear rejection of the traditional use of rhyme and metre, thus leading the way into a new age of free verse which was swiftly taken by such gifted poets as (Syrian) Nizar Qabbani and Adonis and (Palestinian) Fadwa Tuqan.

Some poets such as (Lebanese) Said Aql and Salah Labaki, influenced by the French symbolists, found freedom by turning inward for expression, using often incomprehensible private symbols. They were constantly attacked by the Social Realists for 'useless writing'.

Lebanese poet Yusuf al-Khal returned home after seven years in the United States to found Majallat Shi'r (Poetry Review) in Beirut in 1957. This became the most influential forum for innovative poetry in the Arab world and was strongly opposed to the work of the Social Realists. Poets published in this journal included Adonis and Khalil Hawi who continued to use symbols in their work and also those poets who were experimenting with avant-garde forms by blending classical techniques with dada, existentialist or surrealist forms.

In encouraging the concept of poetry as a unique expression of a personal vision, the Shi'r magazine, by publishing radically innovative work until 1970 and also by publishing the translated work of Yeats, Ezra Pound, Robert Frost, Edith Sitwell and T.S. Eliot and French poets Jacques Prevert and Paul Eluard, continued to influence change.

During the last 15 years, the quest for 'way-out' modern forms has continued, as is seen in the work of many young poets from Mauritania to Oman, while at the same time many poets such as (Saudi Arabian) Abdullah al-Faysal and Husain Sirhan continue to write polished classical poetry.

The Modernist (academic) Yemeni poet Abd al-Aziz al-Maqalih offers a paradox with his exquisitely free yet disciplined use of language, for he can only be described as a classical modernist.

Today rejection of traditional forms and the quest for 'ultra-modernity' among many younger poets can be as obsessive as the denunciation of the work of these poets by some traditionalists.

However, the work of Arab poets of all schools never ceases to fascinate. The extraordinary richness of their language provides the medium for developing unlimited innovation and flexibility of form while maintaining a unique poignancy and vividness of imagery, for poets can choose from an immense vocabulary for symbols, metaphors and allusions to give precisely the nuance of meaning required, often so elusive in other languages. Their language enables them to express the most complicated perceptions in a single line of poetry.

Whatever the outside influences, Arabic poems with a distinctively Arab flavour continue to flow from the pens of poets of all schools. This is particularly evident in western-educated Ghazi al-Gosaibi's evocative poem Oh, Desert (which I insisted on including). The short poems we have selected for our modest volume will, we hope, give readers a taste of Arabic poetry over the past 50 years and show how poets, with a dedication to truth and by drawing on their rich literary heritage, are struggling to maintain their individual artistic integrity and to express an often metaphysical vision of their place in a vastly changing and sometimes tragic world.

Our bridge of poems has been built, poem by poem.

Anne Fairbairn

A note on the translation

ONE OF THE world's greatest masters of translation, Boris Pasternak, was always aware of a deep sense of betrayal of the original text. He wrote in 1933 in a letter to his friend the Georgian poet Titian Tabidze, "... all translations - good and bad - are to a certain extent a violation of the original text, and mine I'm afraid are of the second category." If Pasternak's were of the second category, what would mine be?

To build our bridge of poems, the job had to be tackled, whatever the difficulties. Dr Ghazi al-Gosaibi sent me a liberal rendering in English with each poem to give an insight into the original text. I then took the poems in Arabic with these liberal translations to Kareem Barbara who is from the Sudan and a recent migrant to Australia. He is now an Australian citizen working as the Ethnic Affairs reporter for the Australian Broadcasting Corporation in Sydney.

Kareem and I spent countless hours working together at the dark (for me) coalface of words in Arabic as I tried to absorb the meaning of each poem. Then, alone, I would compose the poems in English, struggling to maintain the original tone, atmosphere and meaning.

When Dr Hussam al-Khatibe visited Sydney in 1987, I read him several of these translations and he said, "They are charming, but they are not the work of the poets."

I tore up my translations, redoubled my efforts, and, with the continuing support of Kareem, started from the beginning. I tried this second time to keep as close as possible to the original text, to maintain the Arabic forms of expression - the music, vitality, ambiguity and imagery; to try to empathise with the poet and to think and feel as the poet felt as he or she was embarking on that vital initial translation - from feeling and perception into poetry. My task was made easier by the fact that I have visited many of the countries in which these poets live. I have observed the ancient landscapes, cities, villages, and the people with their reverence for family life and spiritual values.

With infinite patience and courtesy, Kareem was always available for discussion on the telephone, with a bundle of photocopied Arabic poems in his hand, or for hour after hour talking (sometimes arguing) together.

The poems in English began to take shape. There were areas of interpretation, symbols and allusions still worrying me and I took my problems to Mr Fuad Namour, a Lebanese teacher who was always quietly helpful over many hours of discussion. Then I took the manuscript to Dr M.A. El Erian and Dr Samar Attar who provided helpful insights - Arab poetry cannot be translated word by word: interpretation is all-important.

Finally I flew back to Dr Ghazi in Bahrain to read him the poems in English. I felt he was a little disappointed when he said, "Perhaps the poems we have chosen are too difficult to translate". So when I returned to Australia it was back to square one with infinitely patient and helpful Kareem for the third time.

Pasternak had written to the widow of Titian Tabidze in 1957: "Everything depends on the quality of the translation and even the best translations cannot reproduce what constitutes the essence and charm of the original". Humbled but determined, I began again. If it is impossible to translate, I would try to 'trans-create'. For the poems to 'work' in English, they must to a degree be re-created. Feeling more at ease, I decided to draw even closer to the original text but but I felt free to make the creative changes necessary to capture, as far as possible, in English "the essence and charm of the original".

There have been many difficult decisions to make. For example, when trans-creating classical Arabic poetry, it seemed essential to maintain the feeling of discipline, and this has often meant 'forshortening' the meaning to keep the metre. But in a volume of this kind, when it seems important to highlight different forms of poetic expression, this seemed to be a necessary sacrifice.

The time and effort I have put into this book are my gift to the Arab people, who, with their sensitivity, warmth, generosity and humour, helped restore my faith.

A.F.

Notes

Several of the English poems in this collection have been set in columns to correspond with the classical style of the Arabic text opposite. As with the original text, these are to be read across the columns, not down them.

The designs under each English translation are black and white reproductions of Palestinian embroidery.

FAWZIA

(Excerpts)

Fawzia.
Oh most beautiful among magic names.
Oh music plucked from the lute of a houri*.
Oh most precious pearl, throbbing with humanity.
Oh divine gift from God, filling me with spiritual purity.
Oh eternal source of my love.
Oh Fawzia.
A gentle memory of you flutters into my heart's prayer.
I see you .. I see you, with all your exquisite vitality:
in the beginning of a smile .. dawning;
in the ring of laughter .. golden;
in the embroidery of a pink handkerchief,
fragrant with the treasures
of the gardens of Lahaj*.

Lutfi Ja'far Aman
South Yemen

*Houri – the beautiful women whose companionship is promised in Paradise in the Koran for true believers.
*Lahaj – a province in South Yemen famed for incense.

فوزيّه

شعر: لطفي جعفر أمان

مقتطفات   اليمن الجنوبي

فوزيّهْ
يا أحلى الأسماء السحريّهْ
يا نغماً يعبقُ في قيثارِ حوريّهْ
يا أغلى لؤلؤةٍ نبضتْ إنسانيّهْ
يا دفقةَ ربّ تملأني روحانيّهْ
يا ثروةَ حبّي الأبديّهْ

يا فوزيّهْ
نجواكِ ترفُّ على صلواتي القلبيّهْ
فأراكِ .. أراكِ بكلّ مفاتنكِ الحبّيّهْ
بشروق البسمة .. فجريّهْ
برنين الضحكة .. ذهبيّهْ
بنقوش المنديل الورديّهْ
نسخوكِ كنوزَ عطريّهْ
بجنانِ طيوبٍ لحجيّهْ

IMAGE

His image sleeps in my eyelids.
It wakes with me,
it follows me,
it circles my door.
When I read or write or joke with friends
it's with me.
Before my eyes,
on my book,
in my laughter,
even
in my gloom.

I'm tired of it;
I'm tired of this torture.
If it were paper I'd rip it up.
If stone I'd smash it.

But it is ... myself.

Lame'a Abbas Amarah
Iraq

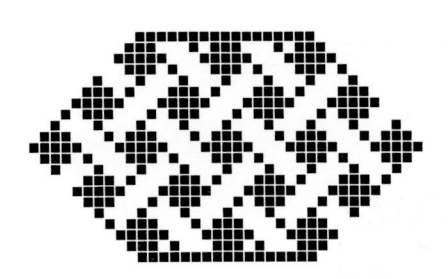

صورتُه
شعر: لميعة عباس عمارة
العراق

صورتُهُ تنامُ في أهدابي
تصحو معي
تتبعني
تحومُ عند بابي
أقرأ، أو أكتبُ، أو ألهو مع الصحاب
وهي معي
وملءُ عيني
وعلى كتابي
في ضحكي
سيان
وأكتأبي

مللتُها
مللتُ من عذابي
لو ورقاً مزقتُها
لو حجراً حطمتُها
لكنها... أعصابي.

KNIGHT IN ARMOUR

The moon living in your eyes
washes the bodies of the dead,
shelters and protects orphans
instilling in them love for their fellow man.
The silence springing from your eyes
raises a grief-stricken mother from her resting place,
watches over thousands killed,
while carrying thousands of shrouds.
The night lying in your eyes
guards the gates of our city,
waiting for the one who will ride from the waves of yesterday
to fold the garment of loneliness and sadness.
The wind beats against the hump of night *
and night drags its garment of silence.
Tears of the grief-stricken mother
water lilies and sweet basil.

Hilal al-Amiri
Oman

* 'Hump' is used to indicate the highest point. The hump of glory indicates the pinnacle of glory.

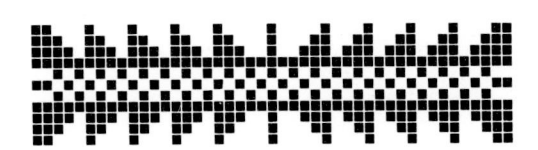

الفارس المدجج
شعر: هلال العامري
(عُمان)

القمرُ الساكنُ في عينيكَ
يغسلُ أجسادَ الموتى
يؤوي الأيتامَ ويحرسُهم
يغرسُ فيهم حبَّ الإنسان
الصمتُ النابتُ في عينيكَ
ينتشلُ الثكلى من مضجعها
يحرسُ آلافَ القتلى
يحملُ آلافَ الأكفان
الليلُ الجاثمُ في عينيكَ
يحرسُ أبوابَ مدينتنا
ينتظرُ القادمَ من أمواجِ الأمس
ويلفُّ رداءَ الوحشةِ والأحزان
والريحُ تدقُّ سنامَ الليل
والليلُ يجرُّ رداءَ الصمت
ويتيحُ دموعَ الثكلى
تسقي الزنبقَ والريحان

YOU, A YACHT AND TO SAIL

You, a yacht and to sail
with winds blowing softly
into our thoughts and into floating fragrances
on mountain tops;
to sail from the violet surface of the sea, at sunset,
which, at a gesture from you, billows into blossom.

You, a yacht and to escape
to the end of the world, from people
the music of the genie and nightrevellers;*
from hills
embroidered with roses and jasmine.
We are searching for a distant harbour beyond this galaxy.

You, a yacht and to land
in the evening – the sky scattered with clouds like pearls –
at a forgotten shore on some star,
resolving,
as we laugh together, all our deepest concerns.
Oh, what ecstasy, what ecstasy.

Sa'id Aql
Lebanon

* Genie: an imperceptible being.
* Sameer: Arabic word for someone who spends the night in festive activity – drinking, singing etc. Nightreveller seems the closest word in English.

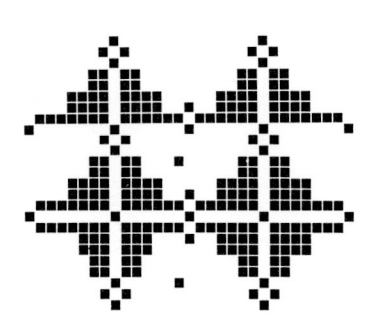

أنتِ واليختُ وأنْ نبحرا
شعر: سعيد عقل
لبنان،

أنتِ، واليختُ، وأنْ نبحرا
في الرياحِ اللينات الهبوب
في التعلّات، وخفقِ الطيوب
في الذرى
مِنْ خضمٍّ ليلكِي الغروب
كادَ مذْ أومأتِ أنْ يزهرا

أنتِ، واليختُ، وأنْ نهربا
آخرَ الأرضِ عنِ العالمينْ
عنْ عزيفِ الجنّ، والسامرينْ
عنْ رُبى
طُرِّزتْ بالوردِ والياسمينْ
نبتغي، خلف السُهى، مطلبا

أنتِ، واليختُ، وأنْ ننزلا
في المساءِ اللؤلؤي الغيوم
شاطئًا نسيًا بإحدى النجوم
حُمِّلا
مذ ضاحكناهُ همَّ الهموم
آهِ، ما أجملَ، ما أجملا

HOMEWORK

"Daddy ..
I feel sorry for the bird in this story!"
I turn towards my little girl;
she's growing up day by day.
She sees letters
as performing dolls;
she sees letters
as glowing wings:
green .. red .. in her evening homework
there's a story about an outcast black duck.

"Daddy ..
I feel sorry for the bird in this story!"
A curtain has lifted, my little one,
and you are wide-eyed with wonder,
while my sense of wonder has vanished –
a curtain has fallen.
You and I are no longer two children;
I've been left alone, searching for
an untrodden moon.
You're surprised that your gentle heart
has been carried by the sad, imaginary bird
towards the shore of tears.

You're growing up, oh Manar.
You have learned that dreams are one thing
and what you see and feel is something else.
You have learned that words are illusion
and for you to feel so sad
there must be suffering;
that we all carry its cross.

واجب المساء
شعر : حسن فتح الباب
(مصر)

بابا .. تصوَّرْ
حُزْني على طيرٍ خرافيّهْ !
والتفتَ القلبُ إليها طفلتي
تكبرُ يوماً بعد يومْ
وتقرأُ الحروفْ
عرائساً راقصةً
وتقرأُ الحروفْ
أجنحةً وضيئةً
خضراءَ .. حمراءَ .. وكان واجبُ المساءْ
حكايةً عن بطةٍ سوداءَ منفيّهْ

بابا .. تصوَّرْ
حُزْني على طيرٍ خرافيّهْ !
وارتفعَ الستارُ يا صغيرتي
أطلّتِ الدهشةُ من عينيكِ
غاصتْ دهشتي
وانسدلَ الستارْ
ولم نعدْ ـ أنتِ أنا ـ طفلينْ
أصبحتُ وحدي باحثاً عن قمرٍ
لم نرقبْهُ أقدامْ
وأنتِ تدهشينَ أنَّ قلبَكِ الوديعْ
يحملهُ طيرٌ خياليٌّ حزينْ
إلى شواطئِ الدموعْ

كبرتِ يا منارْ
عرفتِ أنَّ الحلمَ شيءْ
وأنَّ ما أراهُ .. ما تعنينَ شيءْ
عرفتِ أنَّ الحرفَ وهمْ
وأنّهُ كي تجدني
لابدَّ من عذابْ
يحملهُ على صليبهِ بشرْ

You have learned that love is different from deeds
my little one.
You may be astonished to learn that
we are not alone in our suffering –
the nation suffers.
Her homework was about an outcast black duck.

Hasan Fath al-Bab
Egypt

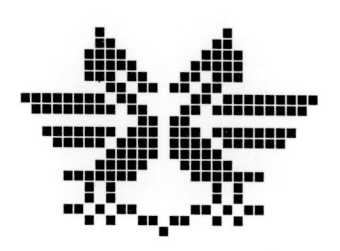

عرفتِ أن الحبَّ غيرُ الفعلْ
صغيرتي
تراكِ تدهشين إن علمت أنّا
لانحمل العذابَ وحدنا
وإنّما الوطنْ
وكان واجبُ المساءِ بطّة سوداء منفيّه

FRIENDSHIP

Reflect ... is what is between us what's between two lovers?
When we meet, are our hands moist?
Do our words dry up and do we both stutter?
Do we both blush profusely?
Do we repeat ourselves again and again?
Asking "How are you?", "Where've you been?", "Where?"?
Do bells ring with the beat of two hearts?
It's as if all happiness exists in the looks we exchange.
Do we imagine the universe is like two eyes?
Seeing only the two of us dancing along the road?
Reflect when you take two steps.
Do you feel against your legs two soft winds?
And your hands, as you walk, have become two wings?
That your breasts are two fiery coals?
Reflect ... is this what's happening to us?
What's between us is still uncertain;
we are two friends .. we're not wildly in love.

My friend .. who knows? We may yet fall in love.
Watch for a spark when our eyes meet.

Shawqi Baghdadi
Syria

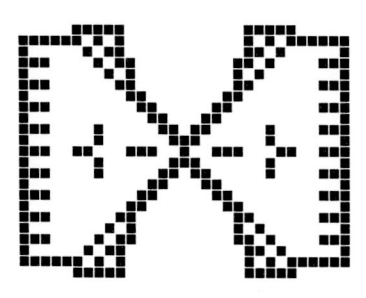

صداقة

شعر : شوقي بغدادي
سوريا

تأمّلي ... أبيننا ما بين عاشقين؟
فإن تلاقينا أيندى الماءُ في اليدين؟
أيَنشف الكلامُ في تلعثم الفمين؟
أيُنشر الدمُ السخينُ ملءَ وجنتين؟
وهل نعيدُ ما نقولُ فوق مرّتين؟
تسألُ "كيف أنت"؟ أين كنت؟ أين؟
أقرعُ الأجراسُ في خفقةِ مهجتين؟
كأنَّ أفراح الوجود وقع نظرتين
وهل نخال كلَّ شيءٍ مثلَ مقلتين؟
لا ترَيان غيرَنا في الدربِ واقفين؟
تأمّلي نفسَكِ إن خطوتُ خطوتين
أتشعرين أن في ساقيك نسمتين؟
وأنَّ في يديك إن مشيتُ جانحين؟
وأنَّ في رافعةِ النهدين جمرتين؟
تأمّلي ... أمثلَ هذا بيننا نزين؟
ما بيننا ما زال في الحنينِ بين بين
نحنُ صديقانِ ... ولسنا بعدُ والهين

أختاهُ ... من يُدريِ؟ فقد نصبحُ مُغرمين
إمّا تكهربنا لدن عينٌ رنتْ لعين

THE BUTTERFLY

She used to come to these anemone dotted fields of wheat
and flutter across grass and trees,
between roses and hearts,
to settle near me.
I would watch as she rose,
my heart following her wings.
As a child I was fascinated by colour
but hers was the first to astonish me.
I ran after her,
all over the place,
leaving our village far behind
as I ran into other villages.
– Life passes like a horse racing through a thread of smoke –
I made many enquiries about her.
The spring and the pomegranate flowers murmured that
she had passed;
they directed me to the mulberry trees,
where, on the highest branch,
she was hanging from a thread, dying.
I clung to this tree
as my life ebbed away.

Hamri Bahri
Algeria

الفراشة
شعر : حمري بحري
(الجزائر)

كانت تأتي لحقول القمح المرشوش بزهر النعمان
وتطير على هامات الأعشاب، وفوق الأشجار
وبين الوردة والقلب
وتحطّ على قرب منّي
أتفرّج ثم تطير
ويطير القلب وراء جناحيها
كانت أول لون يدهشني
وأنا طفل مأخوذ بالألوان
وركضت أطاردها
في كلّ مكان
وتركت ورائي قريتنا
ودخلت قرى أخرى
والعمر جواد يركض في خيط دخان
وسألت كثيرا عنها
قال النبع وزهر الرمّان
مــرّت
وأشارا نحو شجيرات التوت
وبأعلى غصن
كانت تتدلّى من خيط وتموت
وأنا أتشبّث بالشجرة
والعمر يفوت

HER HANDS

As a rhymed line of poetry beginning
or the beak of twilight causes
so I drink up your hands sipping finger
Like clusters of grapes, they confuse the picker,
This one is fuller, its sister softer,
This one seems riper; I'm lost among

They seduce me with their allure .. crying
That one's younger .. this one purer.

"Where are you from?" Her voice, the pulse of a string.
After her question, she was silent, understanding

its cloudy journey, appears and disappears,
the eyes of night to tremble into sleep,
by finger, greedy for a thousand more.
which one is sweeter, which one is clearer?
that one's more tempting, this one more soothing.
the ten; they're beyond all description.

"take me!" – turning away yet wanting me.
In the garden, I don't think there are grapes more transparent.

She moved closer ... "I belong to every exile."
from my answer, my story word by word.

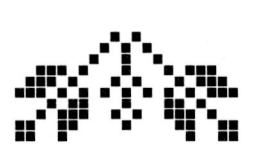

Abdullah al-Baraduni
North Yemen

يداها
شعر: عبدالله البردوني
(اليمن)

مثلما يبتدئ البيتُ المقفّى … رحلةٌ غيميةٌ .. تبدو وتخفي
مثلما يلمسُ منقارُ السنى … سحرًا أرعشَ عينيهِ .. وأغفى
هكذا .. أحسو يديكِ .. إصبعًا … إصبعًا .. أطمعُ لو جاوزنَ ألفا
مثلَ عنقودينِ أعيا المجتني … أيُّ حبّاتهما أحلى .. وأصفى
هذه أملى .. وأطرى أختها … تلكَ أشهى ، هذهِ للقلبِ أشفى
هذهِ أخصبُ نضجًا إنّني … ضعتُ بينَ العشرِ لا أملكُ وصفا

حلوةٌ تغري بأحلى .. كلّها … هتفتْ "كلّيني" وصدّت وهي لهفى
تلكَ أصبى .. تلكَ أنقى .. إنّما … لم أفكّر أنّ في البستانِ أجفى

أنتَ من أين؟ .. كنبضِ وترٍ … ودنتْ شيئًا .. أنا من كلِّ منفى
صمتتْ بعدَ سؤالٍ قرأتْ … من صداهُ قصّتي حرفًا .. فحرفا

THE FACE AND THE MIRROR

As the world sinks into twilight
a legendary woman
emerges from an old testament prophecy, from the books of rivers*
and from painted runes of wizards
on the walls of ancient caves.
From her navel,
the rose-sun of night and day
grows within an azure heart of fire.
She joins in love with sunlight, air and rain,
her womb overflowing with seeds, flowers and fruit.
She embraces the mirror,
dreaming of the river, the horse and the serpent.
She fades into its flat depths,
returning to the books of rivers
and the wizards' brushes in the cave:
leaving behind her little toy,
her broken comb,
the sheen of her green braided hair and sunlight
on the enchanted carpet in the room.

Abd al-Wahab al-Bayati
Iraq

* Books of Rivers: Some ancient Arab stories describe how each great river contained a book (hidden from sight) and that each great river appeared on earth when the hero of the stories in the book, after many adventures, found and held the book. Then the rivers were formed.

الوجه والمرآة
شعر: عبدالوهاب البياتي
(العراق)

العالمُ الغارقُ في الغسقْ
والمرأةُ الأسطورهْ
تطلعُ من نبوءةِ العهدِ القديم وبطونِ كتبِ الأنهار
ومن رسومِ السحرهْ
على كهوفِ العالمِ القديمْ
تخرجُ من سُرّتها
وردةُ شمسِ الليلِ والنهارْ
ولازوردُ النارْ
تمارسُ الحبَّ مع الضياءِ والهواءِ والمطرْ
تحبلُ بالبذورِ والأزهارِ والثمارْ
تحتضنُ المراه
حالمةً بالنهرِ والحصانِ والثعبانْ
وتختفي في قعرِها المطموسْ
عائدةً إلى بطونِ كتبِ الأنهارْ

وريشةُ الساحرِ في الكهوفْ
تاركةً لعبتها الصغيرهْ
ومشطَها المكسورْ
وألْقَ الضفائرِ الخضراءِ والشموسْ
على بساطِ الغرفةِ المسحورْ

FACING DEATH

We all fear death, does fear prevent our death?
I question what's hidden from me but I believe my questions are dead.
Fearing death we avoid walking in cemeteries;
we avoid them through our fear of contagious death.
Do we inherit this fear from our revered fathers or mothers?
What do we fear? Just death, or the unpaved unknown?

Some believe the brave love death. Have you looked into their souls?
Their souls are always light, easily moved by eloquence;
while cowards' souls are heavy, without nobility.

Do those who suicide love death, does death have 'fans'?
Or does hardship so exhaust them, they're tired of what's ahead,
for we're born with a love of life and a wish to live forever.
Every face I've loved will lie beneath the plants;
as death consumes each rosy cheek and charming glance.
Oh my heart, recall the past, oh my eyes, observe around,

of those who've lived in palaces, rotting remains abound
and lips desired in life are earth-kissed in the ground.

Babha Bin Bedaywah
Mauritania

وقفة مع الموت
شعر: بهًا بن بديوه
(موريتانيا)

أَيَرُدُّ المماتَ خوفُ المماتِ؟	كُنّا يَرهبُ المماتَ ولكن
وصَدَّقْتُ كلَّ ظنٍّ رُفاتِ	حدَّثتْني الظنونُ عمّا اختفى مني
نتحاشى المرورَ في المقبراتِ	نحن من خوفِ المنيةِ صِرْنا
نتَّقي العَدْوى من الأمواتِ	نتحاشى المرورَ خوفاً كأنّا
آباؤنا الصِّيدُ عن الأمَّياتِ؟	أَوْرثَنا خوفَ المنيةِ عن
أم مجاهيلَ وَعْرةَ الطُّرقاتِ؟	ما الذي نخْتشي؟ مجردُ موتٍ

أرأيتُم ما في نفوسِ الكُماةِ؟	قد يَظنُّ الكميُّ يهوى المنايا
طِيبُها يَبلغُ التَّبلُّغَ بالكلماتِ	إنَّما أنفسُ الكماةِ خفافٌ
لا تزيدُ العُلى ولا المكرماتِ	ونفوسُ الأنذالِ رُزِحُ ثِقالٌ

يحبّونَ المنايا، وهل لها من هواةِ	أترى من ماتوا انتحاراً
ومَلّوا انتظارَ ما هو آتِ	بل تَضَضَّتْهم الخطوبُ وأضَضَّتْهم
يشتهي أن يعيشَ عُمْرَ الحياةِ	خُلِقَ المرءُ للحياةِ ألوفاً
سوف يَغدو تحتَ الثرى ولِنَيْكِ	كلُّ وجهٍ أحببتَهُ يا فؤادي
وللخدودِ الورديةِ الفاتناتِ	أكلَ الموتُ كلَّ طرفٍ جميلٍ
وانظري مُقلتيْ جميعَ الجهاتِ	فاذكرْ وقلبُ في القرونِ المواضي

كنَّ قبلَ المماتِ في المقصوراتِ	كم جسومٍ هناك صارت سواءً
وكانت تَضِنُّ بالقبلاتِ	وشفاهٍ لعَسٍ يُقبِّلها التُّربُ

DEFIANCE

Tighten my fetters.
Confiscate my papers
and cigarettes.
Fill my mouth with dust.
Poetry is blood in the heart,
salt in bread,
moisture in eyes.
It is written with fingernails,
with eyes,
with daggers.
I shall proclaim in my detention cell,
in the bathroom,
in the stable,
under the lash,
manacled,
in the violence of chains,
that a million birds
on the branches of my heart,
are singing fighting songs.

Mahmud Darwish
Palestine

تحدّ
شعر: محمود درويش
(فلسطين)

شِدُّوا وَثاقي
وامنعوا عنّي الدفاترَ والسجائرَ
وضَعوا الترابَ على فمي
فالشعرُ دمُ القلبِ
ملحُ الخبزِ
ماءُ العينِ
يُكتبُ بالأظافرِ والمحاجرِ والخناجرِ
سأقولُها في غرفةِ التوقيفِ
في الحمّامِ
في الإسطبلِ
تحتَ السوطِ
تحتَ القيدِ
في عنفِ السلاسلِ
مليونُ عصفورٍ
على أغصانِ قلبي
يخلقُ اللحنَ المقاتلْ

AGAINST WHOM?

In operating theatres,
the doctors' masks are white,
their coats are white,
the nurses' caps are white, the habits of nuns,
bedsheets, beds, cotton bandages,
gauze, sleeping pills, the drip,
the glass of milk.
All this weakens me;
all this whiteness reminds me of a shroud.*
So why then, when I die,
will those who come to console
be dressed in the black of mourning?
Is this because black
is the colour signifying deliverance from death?
The colour of a talisman against time?
Against whom?
When was the wild heart safe and at peace?
Between these two colours I receive my friends;
those who see my bed as a tomb
and those who see my life as eternal.
I see in the depths of their eyes
the colour of truth –
the colour of my country's soil.

Amal Dunqal
Egypt

* The shroud (Arabic, kafan) in which the dead in Muslim countries are prepared for burial, is always white.

ضدّ من ؟
شعر : أمل دنقل
(مصر)

في غرف العمليات،
كان نقاب الأطباء أبيض،
لون المعاطف أبيض،
تاج الحكيمات أبيض، أردية الراهبات
الملاءات، لون الأسرّة، أربطة الشاش
والقطن، قرص المنوّم، أنبوبة المصل،
كوب اللبن.
كلّ هذا يشيع بقلبي الوهن
كلّ هذا البياض يذكّرني بالكفن
فلماذا إذا متّ
يأتي المعزّون متشحين
بشارات لون الحداد؟
هل لأنّ السواد
هو لون النجاة من الموت؟
لون التميمة ضدّ الزمن ؟
ضدّ من ؟
ومتى القلب ــ في الخفقان ــ اطمأنّ
بين لونين أستقبل الأصدقاء
الذين يرون سريري قبرا
وحياتي دهرا
وأرى ــ في العيون العميقة
لون الحقيقة
لون تراب الوطن

WEST AND EAST

Praising the beauty of the sun,
           westerners sing:
"How glorious is this day
           with sunshine warming our hearts and minds."
The opposite view is held in the east
           where Arabs sigh:
"You're scorching us, oh sun,
           where are the soft, cloud-bearing winds?"

Muhammad Hasan Faqi
Saudi Arabia

غرب وشرق
شعر: محمّد حسن فقي
المملكة العربيّة السعوديّة

تغنّى بجمال الشمسِ
أقوامٌ من الغربِ
وقالوا .. ما أحلى اليومَ
قد أشمسَ في القلبِ
وقالَ نقيضهمْ في الشرقِ
أقوامٌ من العربِ
لقد أحرقتِ يا شمسُ
فأين نسائمُ السحبِ؟

TUNE 69

I asked about her string of pearls,
"He had a dream of the shores in his mind
He'd return with plunder from summer raids,
as he battled the fury of the breaking waves,
You'd see him at night .. wrapped in the mystery
as though the land rejected and denied him,
At twenty she is filled with love
I asked her for images of the past,
among time's crumbling masonry,
I asked her .. and when I asked her, it seemed
collected by her father, a sailor and fisherman.
as well as a dream of the fathomless depths.
carried by hot winds past cities and countries,
storms near the shoals, hazards and hardship.
of night .. He transformed his life into a journey,
for he was without a home anywhere."
as leaves and flowers are filled with perfume.
fading except for some shadows and threads
filled like a book with mysteries.
I changed her into a singing lute.

Muhammad al-Fayiz
Kuwait

*The title has no special significance

النغم التاسع والستون
شعر: محمد الفايز
(الكويت)

سألتها عن عقود كان يجمعها   أبٌ لها كان صيّاداً وبحارا
رؤى السواحل في عينيه شاخصةٌ   كأنها حمّلت قاعاً وأغوارا
يعود من غزوات الصيف متّشحاً   سموّمَ .. قاطعاً مدناً وأمصارا
يصارع البحر في موج وعاصفةٍ   على الضفاف .. وأهوالاً وأخطارا
تراه في الليل مثل الليل .. متّشحاً   بالغامضات .. أحال العمر أسفارا
كأنما الأرض تأباه وتنكره   فليس يملك في أنحائها دارا
سألتها .. وهوى العشرين يملأها   كما دحا العطر أوراقاً وأزهارا
ولم تعد من رسوم الأمس باقيةٌ   إلا الطيوف ... كما رقعت أطمارا
موزعات على بيت مثلّمةٍ   أحجانُ .. ككتاب ضمّ أسرارا
سألتها .. وكأني حين أسألها   أحيلها نغماً حلواً وقيثارا

DAUGHTER OF SADNESS

Your youth like mine is fading now.
Your world seems desolate without this shadow,
My world's a desert missed by rain,
While thwarted hope brings fond reproach,
as though our drawn-out sighs of longing
With time it seems, our hearts extend
why do you accept to be apart,
When you speak you're so remote
or you avoid speaking as though
I, whose feelings are as delicate
for purest love pervades my mind
No, oh daughter of sadness ... do not
don't withold your love from me,
Your shadowed sorrows haunt my mind
if you remain away for too long
Caravans of lovers visit our garden,
it's unfair to seek refuge in failure now,
love without us would be an illusion

Do I pity you or weep for myself?
who yearns for you with deepest love.
changed from green to barren land.
we're one within our weeping dreams,
bind your suffering to mine.
these overwhelming tides of distance;
trying to keep from my Mihrab?*
as though weak or weary through illness or absence,
evil lurks beneath my clothes;
as early morning's gentle light,
as perfumes drifting through hills and gardens.
fear this poet who loves you .. nor doubt;
the most vivid line in my poetry.
like a series of youthful memories,
you remove the essence of my dreams.
yet we return weighed down with grief;
bowing our heads in bitter defeat;
like wine fermented in lies and deceit.

Abdullah al-Faysal
Saudi Arabia

* Mihrab is the most sacred place of worship in a mosque.

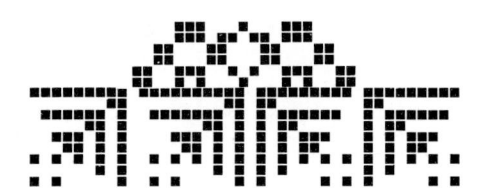

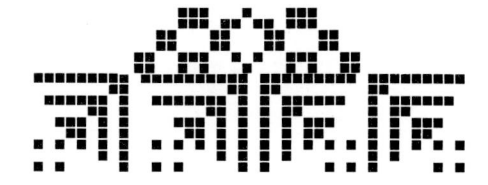

ابنةُ الأحزان
شعر: الأمير عبد الله الفيصل
(المملكة العربية السعودية)

أرثي لِمَابِكَ أم أنوحُ لِمَابي؟	هذا شبابُكَ ضائعٌ كشبابي
يرنو إليكَ بلهفةِ الأحباب	دنياكَ قفرٌ من خيالٍ متّيمٍ
فتحوّلتْ من خضْلِ ليبابِ	ودُناي كالصحراءِ أخطاها الحيا
ما بين حرمانٍ وبين عتابِ	وتشابهتْ أحلامُنا في بؤسِها
شُدّتْ عذابُكَ في وثاقِ عذابي	حتى كأنّ الآهَ من ترديدِنا
ركزاً على مدّ النوى الخلّابِ	وكأنّ قلبينا على طولِ المدى
وتحاولين البعدَ عن محرابي؟	أو بعد هذا تركنينِ إلى الجفا
ضعفَ العليلِ وحيطةَ المرتابِ	وتحدّثيني في وجومٍ خاملٍ
طُويتْ على جسدِ الشرورِ ثيابي	وتحاذرين من الكلامِ.. كأنّما
كالنورِ في وضحِ الضحى المنسابِ	وأنا الذي رقّتْ مشاعرُ قلبه
كالطيبِ بين خمائلٍ ورَوابي	وتعلّقَ الحبُّ الطهورُ بخاطري
من شاعرٍ بهواكِ... أو ترتابي	لا يا ابنةَ الأحزانِ... لا تتخوّفي
سطرٌ أراه مكبّراً بكتابي	لا تكتمي عنّي هواكِ فإنّه
كسلاسلٍ من ذكرياتِ شبابي	وجواكِ طيفٌ حائمٌ في خاطري
تنأين بي عن صبوتي ورغابي	فإذا نأيتِ وطالَ هجرُكِ إنّما
ونؤوبُ من شكوى ومن عذابِ	ويمرّ ركبُ العاشقينِ بروضِنا
وعلى مفارقِنا انكسارُ غِلابِ	فمِن الجنى أن نلوذَ بخيبةٍ
وسُلافةٍ من خُدعةٍ وكذابِ	والحبُّ لولا أنّا توهّمَ سادرٍ

THE MOON AND THE GARDEN

The heart of the garden was running
to hide in the darkness
as the garden drew curtains of shadows to sleep.
The moon swept down;
that royal lover who enjoys the night
climbed the garden wall.
He was half god, half man,*
he was all suffering, and all destiny.
... The garden peered furtively,
surprising him, naked.
– Oh moon,
naked, oh moon;
the deepest sadness is the sadness of truth.
The moon became
a dead stone beneath the garden wall.

Muhammad al-Fayturi
Sudan

* In Arabic the moon is masculine, the sun feminine.

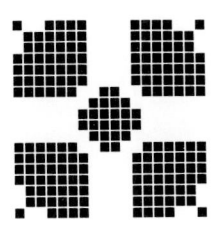

القمر والحديقة
شعر: محمد مفتاح الفيتوري
(السودان)

كان قلب الحديقة يركض
مختبئاً في الظلام
والحديقة أرخت ستائرها كي تنام
وتدلّى القمر
ذلك العاشق الملكي محبّ السهر
ومضى يتسلّق سور الحديقة
كان نصف إله، ونصف بشر
كان كلّ العذاب، وكلّ القدر
... وأطلّت عليه عيون الحديقة
عارياً داهمته عيون الحديقة
ـ يا قمر
عارياً يا قمر
أعمق الحزن حزن الحقيقة
واستحال القمر
حجراً ميتاً تحت سور الحديقة

IN THE CARRIAGE

Stop for a moment, stop.
Order your wheels to stop turning,
during this drawn out time,
Stop, I want to walk,
my feet are tired of riding,
we've been so long together,
If travel's impossible without you
You're a carriage, so I stay stop,
Are you a carriage or a prison?
Stop, let's consider the journey,
You say to think as we travel,
Stop, stop for a moment,
and I'll ask, if you wish, the birds
if they're not to be found and merely
then this prison and its prisoner

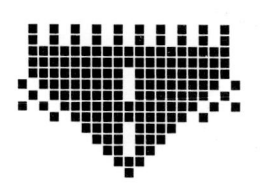

I really must get out.
at least for a little while;
you could vanish for an hour.
to make my way on foot;
can't I walk alone for a mile,
can we separate for a while?
then travelling's not my style.
or perhaps I'd better shut up.
This seems a huge waste of life.
let me choose a different way.
but travel deadens the mind.
I'll rest in the desert shade
or the flowers or streams today;
a mirage can be seen out there,
shall continue on their way.

Muhammad Abduh Ghanim
South Yemen

في المركبة
شعر: محمد عبده غانم
(اليمن الجنوبي)

قِفي بي قليلاً، فإني أريد النزولا	قِفي بي قليلاً، قِفي بي قليلاً
وإن تتوقف حيناً ضئيلا	مُري عجلاتِك ألّا تدور
وإن أوشكتْ ساعةً أن تنولا	ولو ساعةً في الزمان الطويل
على قدميَّ أشقُّ السبيلا	قِفي بي، فإني أريدُ المسير
فما أن تسيران دونك ميلا	لقد سئمت قدماي الركوب
ألا نتفارق حتى قليلا؟	ولم نتلازم طوال الطريق
كرهتُ لأجلك هذا الرحيلا	أما من رحيل بدونك حولي
قفي بي، أوليس لي أن أقولا	أمركبةٌ أنتِ حتى أقول
أعاد الرحيل ضياءً طويلا	أمركبةٌ أنتِ أم أنت سجنُ
وأطلب إن شئتُ عنها بديلا	قفي بي أفكرُ في رحلتي
وهل شلَّ إلا الرحيلُ العقولا	تقولين فكّر خلال الرحيل
لأرتاد في القفر ركناً ظليلا	قِفي بي، قِفي بي، ولوْ لحظةً
وإمَّا الزهورَ وإمَّا المسيلا	وأسأل إن شئتُ إمّا الطيور
وكان البديل بياباً وبيلا	وإن لم أجدها وكانت سراباً
وإن عُدتِ سجناً عُدتِ النزيلا	نواصل مسيرتنا إن أردتِ

YOUR EYES WILL NOT PERCEIVE

Your eyes will not perceive the coming of the season, nor
the joy of thrusting grass.
Your eyes will not perceive trees growing in
the silence of the night, nor the gleam of sap within the leaf.
Your eyes will not perceive the silence of the seed
returning to its closed kingdom.
Your eyes will not perceive returning death,
hiding in its basket all freed birds.
Wrap yourself in the weeds of words
and be assured this world is much larger than your anxious glances.

Muhammad al-Ghazzi
Tunisia

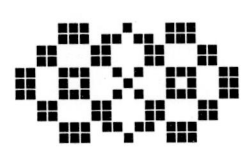

لنْ تدرِكَ عيناك

شعر: محمد الغزي

(تونس)

لنْ تدرِكَ عيناكَ حلولَ الفصلِ ولا فرحَ
الأعشابِ المنبثقهْ
لنْ تدرِكَ عيناكَ الشجرَ الطالعَ في
صمتِ الليلِ ولا وهجَ النسغِ بجوفِ الورقهْ
لنْ تدرِكَ صمتَ البذرةِ عيناكَ
وقدْ عادتْ لممالكِها المنغلقهْ
لنْ تدرِكَ هذا الموتَ العائدَ عيناكَ
وقد خبّأ في سلّتهِ كلَّ الأطيارِ المنعتقهْ
فتخفّ بأعشابِ الكلماتِ إذنْ
وتيقّنْ أنّ العالمَ أوسعُ من نظرتِكَ القلقهْ

THE PEARL

Mine is a distant country, a pearl of the seas.
My country's encircled by water; my hand rests upon it
in the vast azure space
of an extended universe. No power
controls it, no hand except the singing sailor's fist, soaring
like God's star, in a horizon of masts.
My country.
I've tried to read the stars; I've felt safe in this place
as though at my own hearth, as though a wine feast flows in my blood,
as though my caravan of dreams turns the silky sustenance of each day into my purpose for waiting.
Mine is a distant country, so I sought refuge
I say – making an exception for the last time –
in writing a poem about those shores, for the last time.
I'm drawn into a memory of masts.

Qasim Haddad
Bahrain

اللؤلؤ
شعر : قاسم حدّاد
(البحرين)

وطني بعيدٌ مثلُ لؤلؤةِ البحارْ
وطني تُزتِّنُ المياهُ وتستريحُ يدي عليهِ
كأنّهُ سعةُ المدارْ
مستفردٌ في زرقةِ الملكوتِ، لاملكَ
عليهِ ولايدَ إلّا صهيلُ الساعدِ البحريِّ منفلتاً
كنجمِ اللهِ في شفقِ الصواري
وطني
تهجَّيْتُ الكواكبَ واحتميتُ، كأنَّ
ليلتي موقدٌ وكأنَّ مائدةَ النبيذِ على دمي
وكأنَّ أحلامَ الوشيعةِ خبزُ أيّامي وقافلةُ انتظاري
وطني بعيدٌ فالتجأتُ
قلتُ، أستثني لآخرِ مرَّةٍ
وأطوفُ أكتبُ هذهِ الشطآنَ، آخرَ مرَّةٍ
وأصيرُ ذاكرةَ الصواري .

A PREMATURE ELEGY

Two crutches
and two people struggling along an empty road .. only
two shadows and only
these two
with a flickering wick of light dying in the darkness of their eyes.
She said: "the road has worn me out and here I am
creeping bare-footed among the threads of my shroud,
gathering in the days left of my time.
Here I am."
"No .. no."
"Here I am being worn out by the road and by myself.
My face remembers nothing about my face;
my legs have dried up,
my eyes have grown cold,
and my back's hunched under the burden of all that's left of me."
"No .. no, you're still as you were."

She threw away her spectacles, looking
into his eyes.
She gazed deeply into him, her eyes moist with terror
and death. – "You're still the way you were,
you're even lovelier than you were .. as though we'd
lived our lives beyond the years
on this earth and beyond time itself,
so we have not grown old. You haven't."
"Nor you and the warmth of our hands has never lessened."
Two hands clasped two hands.
They smiled in silence,
for the game is still larger than death.

مرثية قبل الأوان
شعر: بُلَنْد الحيدري
(العراق)

عُكّازان
واثنان يدبّان على الدرب المقفر.. إلا
من ظلّين وإلا
من هذين الاثنين
وذبالةِ ضوءٍ تتشرّجُ في دكنةِ عينين
قالت: أتعبني الدربُ وها إني
أتسلّل حافيةً ما بين خيوط الكفن
والملمّ مما أبقت أيامي من زمني
ها إني
كلّا.. كلّا
ها إني أتآكل ما بين الدرب وبيني
وجهي لا يذكر شيئاً عن وجهي
جفّت ساقايا
بردت عينايا
واحدودب ظهري من ثقل بقايايا
كلّا.. كلّا ما زلتَ كما كنتَ

ألقتْ نظارتها عنها.. وأدارت عينيها
في عينيه
غارت فيه... في العين المبتلّة بالرعب
وبالموت ـ أنت ما زلتَ كما كنتَ
بل أروعُ ممّا كنتَ... فكأنّا
ما عشنا عمرينا الآخرَ جُرجَ كلّ سنيّ
الأرض وكلّ الأزمان
فلم نهرم لا أنت
ولا أنت ولم يخفتْ دفءُ يدينا
والتفّت كفّانِ بكفّين
وابتسما في صمت
فاللعبةُ ما زالت أكبر من كلّ الموت

The road divided.
"Shall I say good-bye; I'm going this way alone?"
"Are you saying goodbye; how can I go back alone?
On my two crutches?
How shall I meet death alone?
Stop! Don't go away .. don't go .. don'.."
Two crutches;
the sun sinking in the darkness of a crimson sea
and a woman looking for shade,
the fading shadow of a woman carried along by crutches.
... She is weeping silently.
The silence is as vast as death.

Buland al-Haidari
Iraq

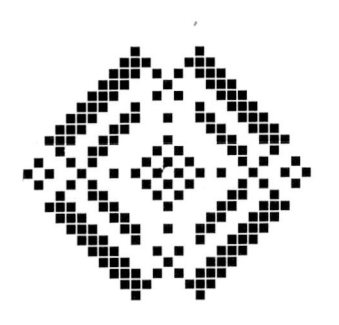

وانشقَّ الدربُ لدربين
أأقول: وداعاً: ها أنذا ماضٍ وحدي
أتقولُ: وداعاً كيف سأرجعُ وحدي؟
وبعكازيّ الاثنين؟
وكيف سألقى موتي وحدي
قفْ! لا تبتعدْ... لا تبتَ... لا
عكّازان
شمسٌ تغرقُ في عتمةِ بحرٍ قانٍ
وامرأةٌ تبحثُ عن ظلٍّ
وبقيّةُ ظلٍّ لامرأةٍ يحملها عكّازان
... وبكتْ في صمتٍ
وكان الصمتُ كبيراً كالموتِ

I TURNED TOWARDS YOU AND PRAYED

(Excerpts)

I'm absorbed in my madness this evening;
you are the evening and you are the madness.
I cross my wound to reach you.
Splendid is this crystal of salt in water
dissolving between you and my dreams.
I'm absorbed in my passion for you to the point of fanaticism.
The flecks of mud in your wound remind me of a nation
whose identity is desecrated.
You are the bridge to a dream
and the dream is you.
You are growth.
You are the talisman .. you are the blending of blood
with the cell.
I renounce all commitments except to you,
renounce .. renounce .. renounce .. renounce,
so take me.
I beg you, for the sake of my passion, not to expose my wounds
and to seek revenge for this crystal of salt
from eyes which have observed, from the beginning, this long thread of events.

'Sarah Harib'
United Arab Emirates

تيمّمتُ صدرَكَ .. صلّيت
شعر : سارة حارب
مقتطفات — الإمارات العربية المتحدة

أمارسُ هذا المساءَ جنوني
وأنتَ المساءُ وأنتَ الجنونْ
وأعبرُ نحوَكَ جرحي
رائعةٌ درّةُ الملحِ حين تسافرُ في الماء
إني أسافرُ بينكَ والحلمِ حتى التلاشي
أمارسُ عشقكَ حتى التعصّب
ذرّاتُ طينِ جراحكَ كالوطنِ
المستباحِ هويّهْ
وأنتَ العبورُ إلى الحلمِ
والحلمُ أنت
وأنتَ التمدّدُ
أنتَ الرقيّ .. وأنتَ التمازجُ بين الدماء
وبين الخليّهْ

صبئتُ بكلِّ إنتماءٍ سواك
صبئتُ .. صبئتُ .. صبئتُ .. صبئتُ
فخذني
أعيذُكَ بالعشقِ أن تستبيحَ جراحي
وتثأرَ من درّةِ الملحِ
من مقلةٍ بينها والبدايةِ خيطٌ طويلْ

BELOVED, I'VE BEEN HERE SINCE MORNING

Beloved, I've been here since morning,
since morning,
composing rhymes and songs,
composing words which are growing
into a new poem
like a palm tree, tall and green, oh, my beloved,
growing towards heaven,
stirring the air as a bee ascending
stirs the air.

Beloved, I've been here since morning,
since morning,
composing words which pierce me from morning until evening.
I brandish my wounds
in the face of a sword slashing crazy poetry;
in the face of a sword slashing the rose and the lemon;*
in the face of a sword defending poems of betrayal.

Beloved, I've been here since morning,
since morning.
I carry in my notebook a garden of daisies;
I carry in my notebook a sailor's compass;
I carry in my notebook a ship of salvation
and a wave from the sea eroding with salt spray the rocks of death.

مِنَ الصَّباحِ جِئْتُ يا حبيبتي
شعر: محمَّد الحارثيّ
(عُمان)

مِنَ الصباحِ جئتُ يا حبيبتي
مِنَ الصباحْ
أحترفُ الأشعارَ والغناءْ
أحترفُ الحرفَ الذي يزرعُني
قصيدةً خضراءْ
كنخلةٍ باسقةٍ خضراءَ يا حبيبتي
تصعدُ للسماءْ
كنخلةٍ تثيرُ قشعريرةَ الهواءِ في صعودها
تثيرُ قشعريرةَ الهواءْ

مِنَ الصباحِ جئتُ يا حبيبتي
مِنَ الصباحْ
أحترفُ الجرحَ الذي يطعنني في الصبحِ والمساءْ
أحترفُ الجرحَ الذي أهنْ
في وجهِ سيفِ الكفِّ بالقصائدِ المجنونهْ
في وجهِ سيفٍ يبترُ الوردةَ والليمونهْ
في وجهِ سيفٍ ينصرُ القصائدَ الخؤونهْ

مِنَ الصباحِ جئتُ يا حبيبتي
مِنَ الصباحْ
أحملُ في دفاتري حديقةَ الأقاحْ
أحملُ في دفاتري بوصلةَ الملَّاحْ
أحملُ في دفاتري سفينةَ الانفتاحْ
وموجةَ البحرِ التي تدكُّ صخرَ الموتِ بالرذاذْ

Beloved, I've been here since morning,
since morning.
Since morning I came like this,
so that you may become a dome to resist the wind;
so that you may become a flower whose fragrance
dispels darkness and shadows,
so children may run about happily.
Beloved, I've been here since morning,
to see morning in your face.

Muhammad al-Harithi
Oman

* The rose is a symbol of beauty; the lemon of growth.

مِنَ الصَّباحِ جئتُ يا حبيبتي
مِنَ الصَّباحْ
مِنَ الصَّباحِ جئتُ هكذا
لكيْ تكوني قبَّةً تقاومُ الرِّياحْ
لكيْ تكوني زهرةً أريجُها
يبدِّدُ الظَّلامَ والأشباحْ
ويجعلُ الأطفالَ يركضونَ في انشراحْ
مِنَ الصَّباحِ جئتُ يا حبيبتي
لكيْ أرى في وجهكِ الصَّباحْ

I WANT TO BE

I want – in your eyes – to be
a rainbow,
which fills you with astonishment, joy
and the ecstasy of madness.
I want to be sustained by your love. To be
the glow in your cheeks and eyes,
more than eyes can see.
I want to be
a road, a forest, a desert.
A veil of shyness.
Lust for revelry.
Fire and rain.
A gesture of farewell.
Dawn's first light.
The journey of winds.
The vast, spreading robe of night.
I want to be,
much more than eyes can see.

Zafir al-Hasan
Lebanon

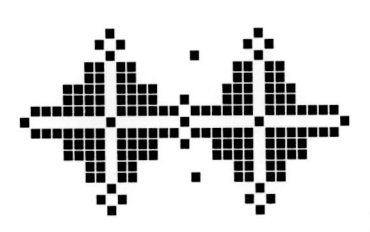

أودّ أن أكون
شعر : ظافر الحسن
(لبنان)

أودّ في عينيكِ أنْ أكونْ
قوسَ قزحْ
يمنحكِ الدهشةَ والفرحْ
ونخوةَ الجنونْ
أودّ أنْ أحيا على حبّكِ. أنْ أكونْ
الوهجَ في الخدِّ وفي العيونْ
أكثرَ ممّا تسعُ العيونْ
أودّ أنْ أكونْ
الدربَ والغابةَ والصحراءْ
إسبالةَ الحياءْ
وشهوةَ المجونْ
النارَ والمطرْ
إيماءةَ الوداعِ في السفرْ
إطلالةَ الضياءِ في الصباحْ
ورحلةَ الرياحْ
ومشّاحَ الليلِ إذا ما أشاحَ الليلُ انتشرْ
أودّ أنْ أكونْ
أكثرَ ممّا تسعُ العيونْ

THE MIRACLE

He grew accustomed to drought, to frost
on his pathway and to closed-in faces.
Suddenly, with the coming of spring,
blossoms and small green leaves appeared;
he wept as he recalled the scent of dark children
and his tears caught fire.

The paralysed man summoned all his strength,
determined to return home and, in his old age, avoid
the depths of loneliness in exile.

Khalil Hawi
Lebanon

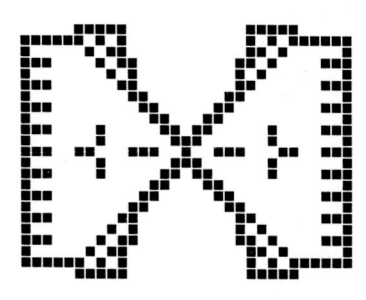

العجيبة
شعر : خليل حاوي
(لبنان)

ألفَ الباسَ مع الصقيعْ
عبرَ الدروبِ، وفي الوجومِ المغلقهْ
هلَّت عليهِ مع الربيعْ
بعضُ البراعمِ مورقهْ
وبكى لرائحةِ الصغارِ السُّمرْ
واشتعلتْ دموعْ

شدَّ المخلَّعُ جسمهُ
ليعودَ، لن يطوي مشيبهْ
في جوفِ عزبتهِ الغريبهْ

THE CITY .. AND I

This is me
and this is my city
at midnight.
The massive square .. walls are ridges
appearing and disappearing one behind the other.
A small leaf, caught up in the wind, spirals to the ground
and is lost along an alley way.
A shadow diminishes,
a shadow grows,
as I walk in the dull glow
of a curious street lamp.
Moved by the memory of a wistful song,
I begin to hum .. I stop.
Who are you, oh .. who are you?
The dumb watchman doesn't understand my story –
since I was kicked out
of my room today
I've been lost, without a name.
This is me
and this is my city.

Ahmad Abd al-Mu'ti Hijazi
Egypt

أنا والمدينة
شعر: أحمد عبد المعطي حجازي
(مصر)

هذا أنا
وهذه مدينتي
عند انتصاف الليل
رحابة الميدان... والجدران تلّ
تبين... ثم تختفي وراء تلّ
وريقة في الريح دارت، ثم حطّت
ثم ضاعت في الدروب
ظلٌّ يذوب
يمتدّ ظلّ
وعين مصباح فضولي ممل
دُست على شعاعه لمّا مررت
وجاش وجداني بمقطع حزين
بدأته... ثم سكتّ
من أنت يا.. من أنت؟
الحارس الغبي لا يعي حكايتي
لقد طردتُ النوم
من غرفتي
وصرتُ ضائعًا بدون اسم
هذا أنا
وهذه مدينتي

ELEGY

When he closed his gentle eyelids and drifted off, I thought
he was sleeping on my lap,
and, like a mother,
I soothed him, alas, with lullabies and prayers,
enfolding him in my love and my shawl.
During the evening, I realised
that divine child, who'd lit up my heart with joy
and warmed me throughout the winter,
was lying in my arms wrapped in the mantle of death.
A cold corpse, heavy in my arms he lay
in eternal silence.

Oh my beloved, I had wished his death would be heroic,
at the hands of others, not ours,
not under our roof.
So why have we, oh you who are departing, why have we let him go
before he enriched our lives with words of farewell?

Muhammad al-Makki Ibrahim
Sudan

مرثية حب طفل
شعر: محمد المكي إبراهيم
السودان

عندما أسبل جفنيه الوديعين وأغفى خلته
نام بحضني
وكأمّ
رحتُ يا ويحي أناغيه بلحني ودعائي
وأغطيه بقلبي وردائي
وتنبهتُ له عند المساء
فإذا الطفلُ الإلهي الذي ضوّأ قلبي بالفرح
والذي أدفأني طول الشتاء
ساكناً بين ذراعيّ وبالموت اتّشح
جثة باردة بين ذراعيّ انطرح
وارتمى صمتاً أبيداً بإزائي

آه يا عيني تمنّيتُ له موتاً جريئاً
وبأيدٍ غير أيدينا
وسقف غير هذا
فلما ذا نحنُ، يا ذاهبةً عنّي، تركناهُ يُولّي
قبلما نخصب عمرينا بكلمات وداع

CRADLE

What is hidden emerges from you;
the dead gather in you.
You stare into the unknown.
You shatter yourself with expectations.
You see the core of things,
yet you don't see me.

I have seen the destruction of things.
The hurricane of time;
corpses of the slain.
Who destroyed the shield of night?
Crept into time
and restored innocence to things?
A tattoo in the corner,
a virgin dancing in the sea;
who put skulls into things?

Sama' Isa
Oman

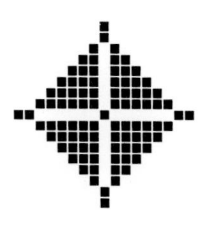

مهد

شعر: سماء عيسى
(عمان)

يخرجُ منكَ المكنونُ
يتواصلُ فيكَ الموتُ
ويحدّقُ في المجهولْ
تتكسّرُ في المأمولْ
تبصرُ لبَّ الأشياءِ
ولا تبصرُني

أبصرتُ دمارَ الأشياءْ
زوبعةَ الوقتْ
أجداثَ القتلى
من حطّم متراسَ الليلْ؟
دلفَ إلى الوقتْ
أعطى للأشياءِ بكارتها

وشمٌ في الزاويةِ
عذراءُ ترقصُ في البحرْ
من أودعَ في الأشياءِ جماجمها؟

THE CRUSHED DOLL

Oh doll that I created and worshipped, as pagans worship a graven image.
Into her I poured my soul, my yearnings, the colours of my dreams, my strange moods.
I made my world in her, she was my wine, my cup, drinking companion and family.
Resting in my dreams, she was lulled by my fragrance .. love .. and my devotion.

Oh doll that I created, then crushed with a giant's hands, this thing I'd made.
Your beauty came from my spell, your fragrance my blood, your allure, my imagination and poetry.
Your lips were inspired by my themes ... oh tiny mouth, moistened by dew and perfumed with the breath of flowers.
My sin made your lips enticing, my shame purified them.
I created you out of my whims of desire, so my whims made you beautiful to me.
Your face was desirable .. only because I left my own transgressions there.
Your eyes did not intoxicate, unless I filled them with all my secrets.
Yet the beauty I created denied me, so my fragrance choked me and my fire consumed me;
denied me to the outrage of passion and poetry, to the outrage of creation and the creator.

I've hurled you back to the humble mud, your garden's without my winds and my storm.
When I left you I left only mud and light and fragrance returned to my soul.

Badawi al-Jabbal
(Muhammad Sulaiman al-Ahmad)
Syria

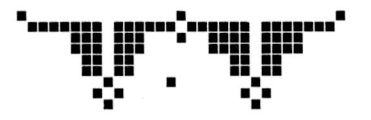

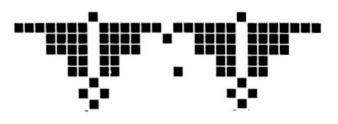

الدُّمية المحطَّمة
شعر: بدوي الجبل
(سوريا)

أيا دُميةً أنشأتُها .. وعبدتُها   كما عبدَ الغاوونَ منحوتَ أحجارِ
سكبتُ بها روحي .. وأهواءَ صبوتي   وألوانَ أحلامي .. وبدعةَ أطواري
جمعتُ بها الدنيا .. فكانت سُلافتي   وكأسي وندمانيَ وأهلي وسُمَّاري
ونامتْ على الحلمِ المريحِ بمقلتي   وهدْهَدَها عطري .. وحبّي .. وإيثاري

ويا دُميةً أنشأتُها .. ثم حطَّمتْ   يدايَ الذي أنشأتُ تحطيمَ حيّارِ
جمالُكِ من سحري .. وعطرُكِ من ديْ   وفتنتُكِ الكبرى خيالي وأشعاري
وثغرُكِ من حاني ... فيا لَلمنَمنَمِ   نديّ بأنفاسِ الرياحينِ معطارِ
ألمْ به إثمي فناداهُ بالمُنى   ومرَّ بهِ وهناً فطيّبَهُ عاري
خلقتُكِ من أهواءِ نفسي ونوّعتْ   بكِ الحسنَ أهوائي وحبي وأوطاري
فما يشتهي خدّاكِ ... إلا لأنني   تركتُ على خديكِ إثمي وأوزاري
وما أسكرتْ عيناكِ إلا لأنني   سكبتُ بجفنيكِ الغوَيّنِ أسراري
أينكرُني حسنٌ خلقتُ فتوْنَهُ   فيخنقُني عطري .. وتحرقُني ناري؟
وتنكرُني؟ يا غضبةَ الشعرِ والهوى   ويا غضبةَ الدنيا .. ويا غضبةَ الباري

رددتُكِ للطينِ الوضيعِ .. وما حنا   على روضكِ الهاني هبوبي وإعصاري
وفارقتُ إذ فارقتُكِ الطينَ وحدَهُ   وعادتْ إلى نفسي عطوري وأنواري

TRANSPLANT OF CONSCIENCE

Doctors have achieved the impossible –
transplanting skulls and hearts and restoring rib-cages.
But when will the banner for their final victory be raised –
transplanting a conscience into minds devoid of conscience?

Muhammad Mahdi al-Jawahiri
Iraq

زرع الضمائر
شعر: محمد مهدي الجواهري
(العراق)

قالوا وقد انتصر الطبيب على المحال من الأمور
زرع الجماجم والقلوب وشدّ أقفاص الصدور
فأجبتهم: ومتى سترفع راية النصر الأخير
زرع الضمائر في النفوس العاريات من الضمير

AWAKENING
– SONG OF A GIRL AWAITING HER FIRST LOVE –

He will come to me .. Here are the roses of resplendent spring,
the glowing daisies   and full-flowing streams.
Tomorrow he will come to me. Oh, what soft magic,
    changing into vapour the cloud of my despair,
        removing all my care.

        So, as my blood stirs within me,
        I feel an awakening of delicious spring,
        overflowing with treasured incense and silk
        in the richness of velvet glory.

There's joy within the tumult of spring   as though at a thousand and one weddings;
as though dreams are gently swaying,   responding to one another softly murmuring,
        arousing my soul and caressing my senses.
        I am moved by a mysterious call

as life flows from the lips of roses   to my sad, responding heart.
        Tomorrow he will come to give life to my dream,
        to whisper my name under the stars,
        to sing longings into the depths of my soul.

The trilling of spring will capture my soul   growing wild in the scented breeze.*
        He will sip the fragrance of my gentle, refreshing love;
        he will dash away the drops of anguish and longing from my cup.

Salma al-Khadra al-Jayyusi
Palestine. USA.

* Zaghradat is a shrill trilling sound made by Arab women as a manifestation of joy.

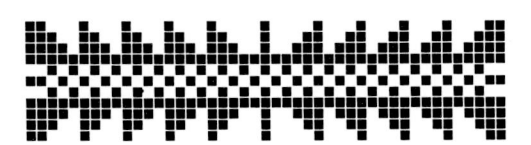

إنبعاث
شعر: سلمى الخضراء الجيوسي
(فلسطين)

أغنية صبية في إنتظار الحب الأول:

سيسعى إليَّ.. أطلَّت ورودُ الربيع البهيّ
ولوَّن زهرُ الأقاحي   وسالت عيونُ الغدير السخيّ
سيسعى إليَّ غداً   أيُّ سحرٍ طريّ
يحيل أثيراً غمامةَ يأسي
ويميعُ همّي
فمن فوحانِ الدماءِ بجسمي
أحسُّ إنبعاثَ الربيعِ الشهيّ
يروّي كنوزَ الشذى والدمقس
ويغرق ذخرَ السنا المخمليّ

وفي جيشانِ الربيعِ حبورٌ   كأنَّ به ألفَ عرسٍ وعرس
كأنَّ به للأماني إندياحاً   تجاوبَ في نغماتٍ وهمس
فأيقظ روحي وداعب حسّي
وهمهمتْ بسرِّ ندائي خفيّ

سرى من شفاهِ الورودِ حياة   إلى قلبي المستهام الشجيّ
غداً سيجي ويوقظ حلمي
ويهمسُ تحت الكواكبِ باسمي
ويُنشدُ الحنينَ بأعماقِ نفسي

وتأسرها زغرداتُ الربيع   معربةً في النسيمِ الشذيّ
فيرشف مني أريج الحنانِ الرقيق النديّ
وينزع من قطراتِ التولّهِ كأسي

APOLOGY TO GOD

How can I pray, oh God?
The words in my heart are no longer
pure and noble.
In the beginning
these words were
innocent and decent,
but today
they're stupid decayed corpses;
emerging from mud,
they're consumed by dragons.

Forgive me, oh God.
In the present age
I don't know how to pray.
Accept, oh God, my suffering as a prayer;
this is all I have.

I hunt birds in fields of words
to cage them in a tower of silence,
so I may release them during the season of thanksgiving and prayer.
But how can I pray
while my mouth is open to the wind
searching for sustenance?
Upon the gates of this era,
in fire and pearls is written:
"man lives by bread alone".

بطاقة إعتذار إلى الله
شعر: الياس خليل جربين
الأردن

كيف أصلّي يا ربّ؟
لم تعد الكلمات بقلبي
بيضاء شريفة
منذ البدء
كانت تلك الكلمات
عذراء عفيفة
أما اليوم
صارت جثثاً خرقاء سخيفة
تنبت في حقل الطين
يمضغها في فمه التّنّين

اعذرني يا ربّ
في هذا العصر لأنّي
لا أعرف كيف أصلّي
واقبل ألمي يا ربّ صلاةً
إنّي لا أملك في هذا العمر سواه

أتصيّد أطياراً من حقل الكلمات
أحبسها في برج الصمت
كي أطلقها في موسم شكر وصلاة
لكن كيف أصلّي
وفمي مفتوح في الريح
أبحث عن لقمة عيش تحيي الإنسان
وعلى بوّابة هذا القصر
مكتوب بحروف من نار وجمان
للخنزير فقط يحيا الإنسان

I know
I'm living in an age of darkness,
but I continue to wander,
searching for this mouthful
in humble cottages and palaces,
so that I may return with my heart uplifted,
knowing how to pray.
Forgive me, oh God
if I fail to find this bread and I don't return,
for I offer my life and my death
as my prayer.

Ilyas Khalil Juryis
Jordan

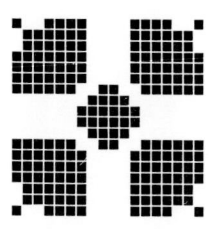

لكنّي أعلمُ
أنّي في عصرٍ مظلمْ
فأظلُّ أدورْ
أبحثُ عن لقمةِ عيشٍ
في أكواخٍ وقصورْ
كيْ أرجعَ مرفوعَ القلبْ
كيْ أعرفَ كيفَ أصلّي
وأعذرني يا ربّ
إنْ لمْ أجدِ الخبزَ ولمْ أرجعْ
فحياتي ومماتي
قربانٌ منْ أجلِ صلاتي

DEATH

Today my friend died;
his eyes are two stars.
I wept over his face
and the place was weeping with me.

The neighbourhood is a picture
of darkness .. No one
kissing,
no one embracing or speaking.
On the pavement here's a bottle
and here two hands
of a man who returns as an echo;
a man passed over by time.

Today my friend died;
his eyes are two stars.

Yusuf al-Khal
Lebanon

موت

شعر: يوسف الخال
(لبنان)

اليومَ ماتَ صاحبي
عيناهُ نجمتانْ
بكَيتُ فوقَ وجهِهِ
بكى معي المكانْ

الحيُّ باتَ صورةً
على السوادِ... لا فمٌ
على فمٍ
لا وجهَ، لا لسانْ
على الرصيفِ ههنا زجاجةٌ
وههنا يدانْ
لعائدٍ مع الصدى
قد فاتَهُ الزمانْ

اليومَ ماتَ صاحبي
عيناهُ نجمتانْ

TWICE

Hind has come to her mother,
she's complaining: "Dawn
and ran away .. then dusk
and fearlessly embraced me,
and his softly-shadowed kohl
I went to the garden this morning,
the garden cried,"oh, my garden!"
So I veiled my face, mother,
surprised, I looked down to see
A rose bush bowed adoring,
and from its topmost branch,
I feared its leaves as they whispered
so I tried to cool off in the sea,
Now wherever I go,
How many boys are drowning
I'm so full of complaints,

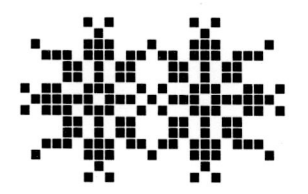

– God's sun and moon together –
kissed me twice today
gave me two braids of his hair
leaving two stars on my lips
across the lids of my eyes.
to avoid each prying glance,
and started to flirt like the rest.
but I felt two hands on my breast;
two pomegranates on me.
twice at my feet
offered me two roses.
two words into my ear
but two waves slapped against me.
these waves are playing with me.
how many are on the brink?
oh God, mother, what do you think?"

Laughing, her mother replies,
"I knew these things one by one,

surprise and pride in her voice:
I've tasted what you've tasted twice!"

Bisharah al-Khuri
(pen name: al-Akhtal al-Saghir)
Lebanon

ذُقْتُهُ مرَّتين
شعر: الأخطل الصغير
(لبنان)

أتتْ هندُ تشكو إلى أمِّها   فسبحانَ مَنْ جمَّع النَّيِّرَيْن
فقالتْ لها إنَّ هذا الضُّحى   أتاني .. وقبَّلني قُبلتَيْن
وفرَّ، فلمَّا رآني الدُّجى   حبَّاني من شَعرهِ خُصلتَيْن
وما خافَ يا أمُّ بلْ ضمَّني   وألقى على مبسمي خَتمتَيْن
وذوَّبَ من لونهِ سائلاً   وكحَّلني منه في المقلتَيْن
وجئتُ إلى الروضِ عندَ الصَّبا   لأخبِّئَ نفسي عن كلِّ عَيْن
فنادانيَ الروضُ: يا رَوْضَتي   وهمَّ ليفعلَ كالأوَّلَيْن
فخبَّأتُ وجهي منهُ ولكنْ   إلى الصَّدرِ يا أمُّ مدَّ اليدَيْن
ويا دَهْشَتي حينَ فتَّحتُ عيني   وشاهدتُ في الصَّدرِ رُمَّانَتَيْن
وما زالَ بي الغصنُ حتَّى انحنى   على قدمي ساجداً سَجدتَيْن
وكانَ على رأسهِ وردتان   فقدَّمَ لي تَيْنِكَ الوردتَيْن
وخِفتُ من الغصنِ إذ تمتمتْ   بأدنى أوراقهِ كلمتَيْن
فرحتُ إلى البحرِ للإبتراد   فحَمَلَني، ونَحْيَهُ، موجتَيْن
فما سرتُ إلا وقد ثارتا   بردٌ فيَّ كالبحرِ رجلحتَيْن
هوَ البحرُ يا أمُّ كمْ من فتىً   غريقٍ .. وكم من فتىً بَيْنَ بَيْن
فها أنا أشكو إليكِ الجميعَ   فباللهِ يا أمُّ ماذا ترَيْن

فقالتْ وقد ضحكتْ أمُّها   وماستْ من العجبِ في بُردَتَيْن
عرفتُهمْ .. واحداً .. واحداً   وذُقتُ الذي ذُقتَهُ مرَّتَيْن

THE STORM

Listen to the gale thundering across the mountains.
Listen to the protracted moaning of the forest.
Listen to all the birds in the darkness;
lost and wet in the torrential rain,
they're searching for shelter until morning.
Who will save them from the slap of the wind?
Open your skylight and look up at the face of the sky;
see it wearing a winter veil
as it hides in fear, behind the clouds.
The wind has blown out the stars.
Close your skylight in the face of the wind   until morning.
Take refuge in me and sleep   oh my darling love.

Salah Labaki
Lebanon

العاصفة
شعر: صلاح لبكي
(لبنان)

اسمعي الأعصار يدوي في الجبال
اسمعي للغاب أنّاتٍ طوال
اسمعي كم طائرٍ تحت الظلام
تائهٍ بلّه القطرُ السجام
يتوخّى مأمناً حتى الصباح
من ترى ينجيه من كفّ الرياح
افتحي الكوّة في وجه السماء
وانظريها لبست ثوب الشتاء
وتوارت رهبةً خلف الغيوم
بعد أن أطفأت الريحُ النجوم
أغلقي الكوّة في وجه الرياح   للصباح
خبّي رأسك في صدري ونامي   يا غرامي

HER FACE AND THE WALL

Between us there are two footsteps.
Two seas – of desire and of terror – are rising,
carrying away the pages of hope.
Everything has changed .. darkness is watching,
preventing a glimpse of our embrace
and an early flowering of our dreams.
All worries have evaporated .. but ours
are not resolved.
They remain like a sign fixed to a wall,
lit up by night and fanned by daylight.
Between us there are two footsteps.
For so long our fingers have been bruised by an imaginary wall
which scatters our weakness in the wind
as remnants of sorrow.
It seems dreaded destiny's preventing the wholeness of things.
Yet your face, a well-spring of mystery,
will remain the source of my fire-tempered strength and courage,
and be my triumph at the final confrontation –
sounding the bell for the exquisite duel.
I draw your face upon the wall;
your image turns green.*
Milk gushes from the wall.
I draw your waist upon the wall;
who taught the wall to dance?
I draw your legs .. I draw ..
across the wall rivers flow and forests grow.
The wall has disappeared!

Hasan al-Lawzi
North Yemen

* Akhdar: Arabic word for green, a symbol of regeneration.

وجهها والجدار
شعر: حسن اللوزي
(اليمن)

بيني وبينك خطوتان
بحران من هلع وشوق يبنوان
ويعلنان تمزق الأوراق في سفر الرجاء
تبدلت كل الجلود... وظل يرصدنا الظلام
ليحول دون عناقنا
وتفتّح الأحلام في الدرب القصير
وتبخّرت كل الهموم.. وهمنا
باق كلافتة على ظهر الجدار
الليل يوقده ويزكيه النهار
وليس يبلغه الشفاء!!
بيني وبينك خطوتان
ووهم جدار طالما أدمى أظافرنا
وبعثر ضعفنا في الريح
أشلاءً من الأحزان

كأنه القدر الرهيب يحول بين تكامل الأشياء
لكنّ وجهك منبع الأسرار
سيظل ممكن بأسى المصقول بالنيران
وهو انتصاري في المواجهة الأخيرة
سيدق ناقوس المنارة الجميلة
وأخطّ وجهك في الجدار
يخضرّ وجهك في الجدار
يباح باللبن الغزير فم الجدار
وأخطّ خصرك في الجدار
من علّم الرقص الجدار؟
وأخطّ ساقيك.. أخطّ..
تقوم غابات وأنهار على صدر الجدار
لم يبق في الأفق الجدار!

NEITHER YOU NOR I

I say happiness lies in dreams,
I see happiness in the shadow of wealth,
Why do I say it can be possessed,
"If it's created, it's created for us."
"I believe happiness does exist."
"This mystery will be solved one day."
"Oh my friend, this is a futile debate,

you claim dreams are man's enemy.
but you see only misery.
while you say it's impossible?
"If it's created, it's not for us."
"Really you shouldn't believe this."
"There is no mystery, there .. nor here."
neither you .. nor I know the truth at any rate."

Iliya Abu Madi
Lebanon. USA.

لا أنتَ ولا أنا

شِعر: إيليا أبو ماضي (المهجر)

قلتُ: السعادةُ في المنى، فرددتني	وزعمتَ أن المرءَ آفتُه المنى
ورأيتُ في ظلِّ الغنى تمثالها	ورأيتَ أنتَ البؤسَ في ظلِّ الغنى
مالي أقولُ بأنها قد تقتني	فتقولُ أنتَ بأنها لا تُقتنى
وأقولُ: إن خُلقتْ فقد خُلقتْ لنا	فتقولُ: إن خُلقتْ فلم تُخلقْ لنا
وأقولُ: إني مؤمنٌ بوجودها	فتقولُ ما أحراكَ أن لا تؤمنا
وأقولُ: سرٌّ سوفَ يُعلنُ في غدٍ	فتقولُ: لا سرَّ هناك.. ولا هنا
يا صاحبي، هذا حوارٌ باطلٌ	لا أنتَ أدركتَ الصوابَ.. ولا أنا

FROM THE RUBAYI'T OF SINBAD

Can a man be other than himself?
How would night seem without revelry?
Could a true poet live without feeling?
How does a face appear when it's put on?

Dearest friend,
I'm tired of travelling from place to place;
I've criss-crossed the world
without finding an oasis
to shelter my soul from stares of hate.
All eyes, oh my friend, reject me with a look which says:
"Alien, go home!"

Night follows day;
each day is as dark as night,
dark and gloomy,
while Sinbad, as I know him,
remains an alien.

Dearest friend,
Sinbad is returning home
with only half his soul.
Restore his soul,
and dress his wounds.
Who other than you, most precious one,
is able to heal wounds?

Haydar Mahmud
Jordan

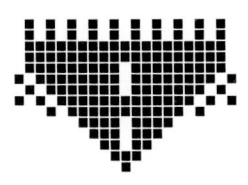

من رباعيات السندباد
شعر: حيدر محمود
الأردن

هل بمُلكِ الإنسانُ أن يكونَ غيرَ نفسِهِ؟
كيف يكون الليلُ لو كان بلا سَمّار؟
هل يستطيعُ الشاعرُ الشاعرُ أن يحيا بغيرِ حِسّهِ؟
كيف يكون الوجهُ عندما يكون مُستعارًا؟

صديقتي:
تعبتُ من تنقّلي بين فجاجِ الأرضْ
قطعتُها واحةً في إثرِ واحدةْ
فلمّا ألقى واحةً
تحمي دمي من العيون الحاقدة
كلُّ العيون، يا صديقتي، ترمقني بالرفضِ
عُدْ يا غريبْ!

الليلُ يتبعُ النهار
والنهارُ كالحٌ كالليلِ
كالحٌ كئيبْ
والسندبادُ مثلما عرفتَه
يظلُّ دائمًا غريبْ

صديقتي:
السندبادُ عائدٌ إلى الحِمى
بنصفِ روحْ
رُدّي عليه روحَه
وضمّدي جروحَه
فمَن سواكِ يا أعزَّ الناسِ
يضمّدُ الجروحْ؟

I LOVE YOU ... HOW SHOULD I LOVE YOU?

(Excerpts)

I am still searching among meanings
and among Arab encampments.
I am still searching
among the lineage of each ancient alphabet.
I've flicked through the pages of my diaries about love.
I've turned all the tribes against me.
I've plunged into poetry
even contemporary and foreign.
I've searched among ruined kingdoms in Egypt, Rome and the land of Hijaz.*
I've even looked into all the tombs of lovers.

I'm still searching but
all forms of expression have been used up by those long dead;
all forms of expression have been trampled on by passers-by.
I've found nothing on my way to express my feelings;
to express my love for you,
why I love you,
how I love you .. I do love you,
how you've penetrated every vein
pulsing under my skin.
How you've become my eyes;
how you've become my tongue.
How my feelings fade at night when you fall asleep
and stir when you wake.
For me your glow transforms darkness into light
and into a glittering river of Kawther *
with every throb of my heart.

I have seen nothing along the way
except "I love you", oh all my soul.
All words spring up in awe before you
and kneel adoring on the ground
whenever you appear.

Ali Mirza Mahmud
Qatar

* Hijaz: Eastern province in Saudi Arabia
* Kawther: Abundant river in Paradise flowing with sweet water.

أحبّك.. كيف أحبّك
شعر: علي ميرزا محمود
(قطر)

مقتطفات

ما زلتُ أبحثُ بين المعاني
وبين مضاربِ باحاتِ العربيّة
ما زلتُ أبحثُ
بين سلالاتِ كلِّ الحروفِ العريقةِ في الأبجديّة
قلّبتُ كلَّ دفاترِ عشقي
وأنسبةَ كلِّ القبائلِ ضدّي
وغصتُ جميعَ البحورِ
حتى البحورِ الحديثةِ والأجنّة
بين ممالكِ عشّاقِ مصرَ وروما وأرضِ الحجاز
بين قبورِ جميعِ المحبّين أدخلتُ رأسي

وما زلتُ أبحثُ لكنْ
كلُّ التعابيرِ قد مجّها الذاهبون
وكلُّ التعابيرِ قد داسها العابرون
ولم أرَ في الدربِ شيئاً يعبّرُ عنّي
يعبّرُ عمّا أحبّك
فيمَ أحبّك
كيفَ أحبّك .. إنّي أحبّك
كيفَ تغلغلتِ في كلِّ عِرقٍ
يضجّ وينفرُ من تحتِ جلدي
كيفَ عيوني أصبحت
كيفَ لساني قد صِرت
كيفَ الأحاسيسُ لمّا تموتُ مع اليلجينَ بنا
تحيا على وقعِ حسِّك
فيها سناكِ يحيلُ الظلامَ نهاراً
ونهراً من الكوثرِ الدرّ
في كلِّ خالجةٍ من فؤادي

لم أرَ في الدربِ شيئاً
غيرَ احبّك، يا كلَّ روحي
يا من جميعُ الحروفِ تخرُّ جلالاً على وجنتيك
وتهوي على الأرضِ ساجدةً
حينَ تأتينَ بين يديك.

FEAR

A small word
is spoken or written on water
or winds carry it or sands spread it in the desert.
It comes into being and is crafted
by accidents of noise and tumult.
A small word,
nourished by the sun's rays at midday,
can grow in the atmosphere,
veiling the face of the sun .. casting its shadow
to drown me in echoes of the past.
Why does it?
My kingdom: a kingdom of silence,
so shut up.
I hate any word used for purposes other than praise or ridicule.*

Ahmad al-Majati
Morocco

* Madh is an Arabic word for a form of panegyric. Hijaa is a word used to describe ridicule in poetry, used by poets to mock one another.

الخوف

شعر: أحمد المجاطي

المغرب

الكلمةُ الصغيرةُ
تُقالُ او تخطفُ فوقَ الماءِ
تمضي بها الرياحُ، أو تبثُّها الرمالُ في الصحراءِ
تولدُ، او تكونُ، او تصوغُها
مصادفاتُ الصخبِ والضوضاءِ

الكلمةُ الصغيرةُ
يمدُّها الشعاعُ او تمدُّها الظهيرةُ
ما بالها تكبرُ في الهواءِ
تحجبُ وجهَ الشمسِ... تلقي ظلَّها
تغرقُني بالرجعِ والأصداءِ

ما بالها؟
مملكتي: مملكةُ الصمتِ
أخسأوا
أمقتُها كلمةً قيلَت لغيرِ المدحِ والهجاءِ

SILENCE

Do you know the value of silence,
when the ink dries in our inkwell
and words die on our lips
and we fear to say .. no,
hoping others will say .. no,
rejecting silence.

Who demolishes houses
and breaks down boundaries and barriers?
Who fills words with explosives
and who fires poems
at palace peaks and dung heaps?
Who conquers fortresses and temples,
with his fighting poems?

Gold will fall from the sky like rain,
children dance in the street
and holy shrines bow down to us.

Ja'far Majid
Tunisia

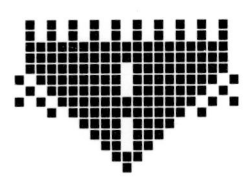

الصَّمت
شعر: جعفر ماجد
(تونس)

هل تعرفون قيمة السكوت
حين يجفُّ الحبر من دواتنا
والحرف في شفاهنا يموت
حين نخاف أن نقول.. لا
ونشتهي لو غيرنا يقول.. لا
ويرفض السكوت

من يهدم البيوت
ويكسر الحدود والفواصل
من يملأ الحروف بالقنابل
ويقذف القصائد
على ذرى القصور والمزابل
من يفتح الحصون والمعابد
بشعر المقاتل؟

ستُمطر السماء بالذهب
ويرقص الأطفال في الشوارع
وتنحني أمامنا الصوامع

ELEGY FOR A WOMAN OF NO CONSEQUENCE

She has gone. No one looks pale and no lips are trembling.
The news of her death is not repeated from door to door.
There are no sorrowing windows, so no curtains are parted
for eyes to follow her coffin until it is out of sight.
Only her remains, shaken by memory, are carried along the road.
Finding no echo of response, word of her death
seeks refuge in oblivion, in an abyss
whose sadness is mourned by the moon.

Carelessly night is yielding to day.
With first light comes the cry of the milk woman, pangs from fasting,
mewing of starving, slap-sided cats,
squabbling street-hawkers, bitterness and struggle;
kids hurling pebbles at one another across the road,
filthy water seeping into gutters along narrow lanes; while the wind
plays a lonely game with a roof-top door
in a half-real world.

Nazik al-Mala'ikah
Iraq

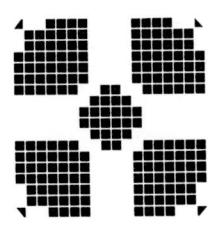

مرثية إمرأة لا قيمة لها
شعر: نازك الملائكة
(العراق)

ذهبت ولم يشحب لها.. خدٌ ولم ترتجف شفاه
لم تسمع الأبواب قصة موتها تُروى وتُروى
لم ترتفع أستارُ نافذةٍ تسيل أسىً وشجوا
لتتابع التابوت بالتحديق حتى لا تراه
الا بقية هيكل في الدرب ترعشه الذكر
ثم اغترف في الدروب فلم يجد مأوى صدهْ
فأوى إلى النسيان في بعض الحفر
يرثي كآبته القمر

والليل أسلم نفسه.. دون إهتمام للصباح
وأتى الضياء بصوت بائعة الحليب وبالصيام
بمواء قطٍ جائع.. لم يبق منه سوى عظام
بمشاجرات البائعين، وبالمرارة، والكفاح
يتراشق الصبيانُ بالأحجار في عرض الطريق
بمسارب الماء الملوّث في الأزقّة، بالرياح
تلهو بأبواب السطوح بلا رفيق
في شبه نسيانٍ عميق

THE PEASANT

Generously, he pays his debts to life, with debts to him unpaid until now.
He goes on and on, cleaving the soil, unfailing resolve etched on his brow.
His eyelids close as the sweat of toil is flowing down to blur his vision.
Look closely at his forehead; see how many pearls are gleaming.
His eyes withold their tears it is his forehead weeping.

Shafiq al-Ma'luf
Lebanon.

الفلاح

شعر: شفيق معلوف
(المهجر)

وفَّى الحياةَ ديونَها كرماً	وما وفيت ديونه
ومضى تشقُّ الأرضَ قبضتُه	بعزمٍ لا يخونه
عرقُ الجهادِ همى على	عينيه، فانطبقت جفونه
هلّا نظرتَ جبينَه	كم فيه لؤلؤٌ تزينه
ضنَّت عليه بالدموع	عيونُه فبكى جبينه

A SONG FOR ASHES
FOR A MAN WHO WAS MY FRIEND

Before you withdraw this dagger thrust into
my back .. let me look at you,
for my blood, embracing it, sniffed on the blade
something of you, sensing a shadow of our old embrace
and the fading fragrance of friendship.

The claw of a wolf .. and the palm are the same,
the palm of the friend I carried in my eyelids*
and my tears sustained.
For him I was feathers and the horizon.*
For him I was escape from silence.
For his sake I fought against tempest and fire.
I shared words with him.
Why have I become ashes in his view
so we've both disappeared?
Roses and thorns are the same,
as are a poem and a wound.
How has my apple – alas – become a stone?*

Who will share with me the ecstasy of God,
emerge from the mouldering present .. from the bread of desolation
and brave a tempest of ashes?
Who will don trees of nothingness,
bite the bitter fruit of brotherly remorse
and escape from this world of paper faces?

Abd al-Aziz al-Maqalih
North Yemen

* A sign of extreme affection
* Freedom and space. "Feathers and the Horizon" – the title of this book.
* Growth and non-growth

أغنية للرّماد
إلى الذي كان صديقي
شعر: عبد العزيز المقالح
(اليمن)

قبلَ أنْ ترفعَ الخنجرَ المتوغّلَ
في الظهرِ.. دعني أراكَ
فإنَّ دمي حين عانقَه، شمَّ في نصلِه
مقطعاً منكِ، أدركَ إيماءةً للعناقِ القديمْ
وأدركَ آثارَ رائحةٍ للصداقةْ

يستوي مخلبُ الذئبِ.. والكفُّ
كفُّ الصديقِ الذي حملته جفوني
ورواه دمعي
وكنتُ له الريشَ والأفقَ
كنتُ النجاةَ من الصمتِ
ناوشتُ من أجلِه الريحَ والنارَ
قاسمته الكلماتِ
لماذا ترمّدَ وجهي في وجهِه
وإختفينا
استوى الزهرُ والشوكُ
والشعرُ والجرحُ
كيف استوتْ ـ آه ـ تفّاحتي والحجر

مَنْ يقاسمني نشوةَ اللهِ
يخرجُ من عفنِ الوقتِ.. من خبرِ هذا الخرابِ
ويدخلُ في عصفِ هذا الرمادِ
ومَنْ يرتدي شجراً من هباءْ
ويقصمُ حنظلةَ الندمِ الأخويّ
ويرحلُ عن عالمٍ ورقيّ الوجوهْ؟

A PEN

The doctor listened to my heart;
he asked:
"Is the pain here?"
"Yes", I replied.
With a scalpel he sliced open the pocket of my jacket,
removing a pen.
The doctor shook his head .. and leaned forward, smiling.
He said,
"This is only a pen."
"No sir," I argued,
"It is a hand and a mouth
a bullet and blood.
It openly accuses –
marching forward without feet."

Ahmad Matar
Iraq

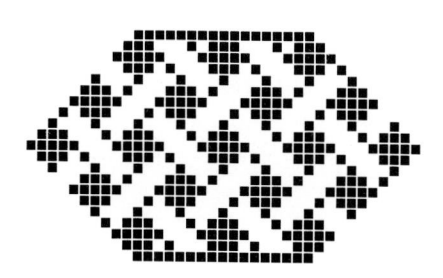

قلم
شعر: أحمد مطر
«العراق»

جسّ الطبيبُ خافقي
وقال لي:
هل هاهنا الألمْ؟
قلتُ له نعم
فشقّ بالمشرط جيبَ معطفي
وأخرج القلمْ
هزّ الطبيبُ رأسه... وسأل وابتسمْ
وقال لي:
ليس سوى قلمْ
فقلتُ لا يا سيدي
هذا يدٌ وفمْ
رصاصةٌ ودمْ
وتهمةٌ سافرةْ
تمشي بلا قدمْ

GARMENTS OF THE SOUL

Each day I discard garments, those tattered beliefs of the past,
hoping to bare my soul of veils degrading me.
Yet as I remove each garment, a thousand cling to me,
so I'm always taking them off, as though garments constitute me.
I'm afraid to remove them all, for I may not find my soul.
Layer upon layer upon layer, it seems .. an onion's like me.

Ahmad al-Safi al-Najafi
Iraq

أثواب الروح

شعر: أحمد الصافي النجفي
(العراق)

كلُّ يومٍ أزيحُ عنّي ثوباً .. بالياً من عقائدِ الأحقابِ
أملاً أن أعرّي النفسَ حقّاً .. من لباسٍ يشينُها وحجابِ
غيرَ أنّي إن أنضُ ثوباً أصادفْ .. ألفَ ثوبٍ ملاصقاً لإهابي
فتراني ما عشتُ أنزعُ أثواباً .. كأنّي كوّنتُ من أثوابِ
صرتُ لأخشى إن أنضُ كلَّ ثيابي .. لمَ أصادفْ روحاً وراءَ الثيابِ
فكأنّي القشورُ كوّنَ منها .. بصلٌ... ما بهِ سوى الجلبابِ

BURNING LETTERS

Love's tender blaze has faded.   I've finished with its pain.
Yet sometimes I feel I'm dying   from emotions that remain
when memories return to haunt me, swarming in my mind.
One long, ugly night when darkness banished sleep,
I thought of her letters resting   like a child as it dreams;
with time they'd grown as dark   as clouds filled with rain.
They shall not rest I swore   they shan't enjoy such peace.
I burned them; flames consuming   the precious remnants of love,*
obliterating our story,   with all it contains.
I burned my soul with them, in the core of those flames.
The ashes of my passion mourn on the ashes of her passion.

Ibrahim Naji
Egypt

* Taraa is an Arabic word for grazing. When camels or sheep graze, they consume every type of grass, leaves and weeds.

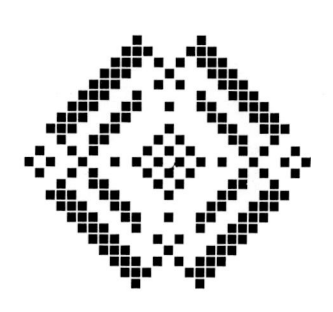

رسائل محترقة
شعر: إبراهيم ناجي
(مصر)

ذوتِ الصبابةُ وانطوتْ وفرغتُ من آلامِها
لكنني ألقى المنايا من بقايا جامِها
عادتْ لقلبي الذكرياتُ بحشدِها وزحامِها
في ليلةٍ نكراءَ أرقَني طويلُ ظلامِها
نامتْ رسائلُ حبِّها كالطفلِ في أحلامِها
زرقاءَ صيَّرها البِلى كسحابةٍ بغمامِها
فخلفتْ لا رقدتْ ولا ذاقتْ نشىَّ منامِها
أشعلتُ فيها النارَ ترعى في عزيزِ حطامِها
تغتالُ قصةَ حبِّنا من بدئِها لختامِها
أحرقتُها، ودميتُ قلبي في صميمِ ضرامِها
وبكى الغرامُ الأدمعي على رمادِ غرامِها

WINDOWS

Windows:
first step towards the world,
song over a vast sea of clouds,
a voyage.
Windows:
a rose,
braided moonlight spreading over hills.
Windows:
a pulse in the darkness of passing night.
Chains and the men.
Windows:
a way to heaven for the prayers of the lonely girl next door,
oasis for lovers, children
and baskets of ripe fruit.
Windows:
sailor's seagull flying over
the drowsy heart.
Windows:
the wisdom of stone, emerging from the centre of silence,
approaches mountain peaks.

Ibrahim Nasrallah
Palestine

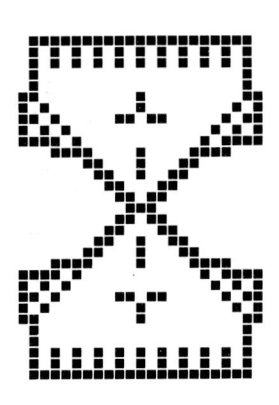

النوافذ

شعر: إبراهيم نصر الله
(فلسطين)

النوافذ
خطوةٌ أولى إلى الدنيا
وأغنيةٌ على غيمٍ فسيحٍ
وارتحالْ

والنوافذ:
وردةٌ
وجدائلُ القمرِ الموزّعِ في التِلالْ

والنوافذ:
نبضةٌ في عتمةِ الليلِ المسافرْ
في السلاسلِ والرجالْ

والنوافذ:
سُلّمُ الصلاةِ جارتِنا الوحيدة
واحةُ العشّاقِ والأولادِ
والثمرُ الذي يأتي شهيّاً في السلالْ

والنوافذ:
نورسُ البحّارِ في القلبِ
الذي أغفى ومالْ

والنوافذ:
حكمةُ الجدرانِ أن تخرجَ من صدورِ الصمتِ
نحوَ ذُرى الجبالْ.

IN HOSPITAL

Gift of Lilies

Lilies from your sweet hands,   derive their mystery from you.
Their beauty's stolen from yours;   their enchantment increased by yours.
In them I find your charm   and from them I breathe your fragrance.
I caress .. and kiss each one,   to reach your mouth in lily-mouths.

I Had a Heart

Once my heart was young,   filled with romantic dreams.
But my heart's been damaged by fires of love .. and melted.

Oh Doctor!

Oh doctor! Be gentle with my tired heart .. no longer
                      can it support my sorrow.
Nothing can comfort or strengthen it now,
                      except the merciful doctor's scalpel.

Isa al-Na'uri
Jordan

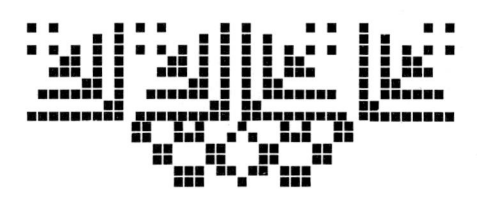

في المُسْتَشْفى
شِعر: عيسى الناعوري
(الأردن)

هديّة الزنبق

الزنبقُ مِنْ يدِكِ الحلوةِ   يجلو أسرارَك في سرّهِ
مِنْ خدّكِ يأخذُ فتنتَه   ويُضاعفُ سحرَكِ من سحرِهِ
إنّي أتملّى حُسنَكِ فيه   وأنشقُ عِطرَكِ من عِطرِهِ
وأداعبُه .. وأقبّلُه   كي ألثمَ ثغرَكِ في ثغرِهِ

كان لي قلب

كانَ لي قلبُ فتًى   عاشَ أحلامًا عذابا
غيرَ أنّ القلبَ قد أتلفَه الحبُّ .. فذابا

يا طبيبي !

يا طبيبي ! رفقًا بقلبي .. فقلبي
لم يعدْ قادرًا الحملَ همومي
لم يعدْ ما يريحُه أو يقوّيه
سوى مبضعٍ للطبيبِ الرّحيمِ

HER DAUGHTER

I believed I'd buried all thoughts of love,
but destiny drew us together .. one day,
fresh in her innocence like a breath from the hills,
This child the dearest replica,
How has this happened .. she inherits
even the fall of hair, the pursed
Oh, her little face after
Has her daughter followed her,
It's ten years since we loved each other;
Once more the image of her mother,
Weeping, I catch her in my arms,

that those barking storms had died for good,
when she fluttered towards me, a wild butterfly,
her adorable smile from Fatiha.*
after such a painful separation.
even the charm of that singing lisp;
mouth, even the absent look.
this absence shocks me through and through.
to remind me of her absent mother?
it seems like yesterday to me.
elegant .. noble .. sings in my blood.
doesn't she have her mother's perfume?

Nizar Qabbani
Syria

* The opening Sura of the Holy Koran.

طِفلتها

شعر: نزار قباني ـ سوريا،

طَالَعَنى دَربي… بِهَامَةٍ	ترفُّ كالفَراشَةِ الجامِحَه
طفولةٌ كما تَبوحُ الرُّبى	ومَبسِمٌ كأنّه الفاتِحَه
وكنتُ شيّعتُ زمانَ الهوى	وانطفأتْ زوابعٌ نابِحَه
يا صِغرَها، أعزَّ أنموذجٍ	من بعدِ تلكَ الغربةِ الفادِحَه
وكيفَ هذا كانَ… قد وُرِثْتُ	حتى رَنينِ اللغةِ الصادِحَه
حتى انثيالَ الشَّعرِ حتى الفمِ	الملمومِ، حتى النظرةِ السارِحَه
يا وجهَها الصغيرَ.. غِبَّ النَّوى	نفضتني جارحةً جارِحَه
هل أقبلتْ طفلتُها بعدها	تفجعُني بأمِّها النازِحَه
عشقتُ أعوامَ على حبِّها	كأنَّهُ في الليلةِ البارِحَه
ولم تزلْ صورتُها في دَمي	عريقةً.. أنيقةً… سابِحَه
أخذتُها مقبلاً.. باكياً	أمَا بِها من أمِّها رائِحَه

SUITCASE

Its ceiling is low;
between its walls
a warm eternity.
Shall I say, then, this is my home?
Well,
I have no other home.
I have no other.

Samih al-Qasim
Palestine

الحقيبة
شعر: سميح القاسم
(فلسطين)

سقفها واطئٌ
بين جدرانها
أبدٌ دافئٌ
هل أقولُ إذن إنها منزلي؟
حسنًا،
ليس لي منزلٌ غيرها
ليس لي

TO WHOM THE GLORY?

Glory in life belongs to the man who buys life
with all he has – his food, his joy, his blood;
to the man who pours fragrant essence
from his soul and heart,
from the flames of suffering.
Glory in life is complete for the one who dies
for a principle, for an ideal, for a grain of sand.
For the voice of a bird
in the gardens of his homeland.
For a girl whose face is washed with tears.
For the smile that lights up the face of an old father.
For the lisp of a small child.
For the laughter of a river.
For a tent pulled this way and that by evening winds.
For a seed sprouting high on a mountain side.

Hasan Abdullah al-Qurashi
Saudi Arabia

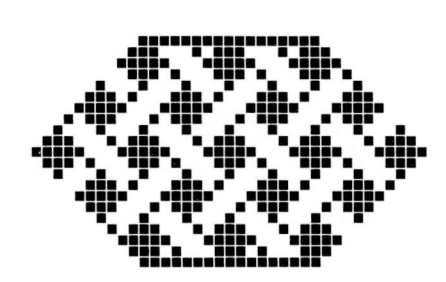

# لِمَنِ المجد؟
شعر: حسن عبدالله القرشي
(المملكة العربية السعودية)

المجدُ في الحياةِ حقٌّ مشتري الحياةْ
بكلِّ ما يملكُ، بالقوتِ، وبالفرحةِ، بالدماءْ
لِمن يوزِّعُ النَّدى ويهرقُ الطيوبْ
من روحهِ مِنْ قطراتِ قلبهِ
من وقدةِ العذابْ
المجدُ في الحياةِ خالصًا لِمن يموتْ
لبلدٍ، لفكرةٍ، لذرَّةٍ من التُّرابْ
لصوتِ طيرٍ هزجٍ
في أيكةَ الوطنْ
لغادةٍ تغسلُ وجهَها الدموعْ
لبسمةٍ تلوحُ في محيَّا والدٍ عجوزْ
للثغةٍ في شفةِ الطفلِ
لضحكةِ النهرْ
لخيمةٍ تجذبُها الرياحُ في المساءْ
لمولدِ النبتةِ في مطارفِ الجبالْ

OH DESERT

I've searched the world .. without finding
land more barren,
love more pure,
or rage more fierce than yours.

I came back to you, oh desert,
sea-spray on my face;
in my mind, a mirage of tears,
a shadow moving in the sea before dawn
and a golden flash of braided hair.
On my lips, two lines of poetry –
a song without echo.

I came back to you, disenchanted.
I've found there's
no trust between human beings.
I came back to you deprived;
the world's like a rib cage
without a heart.
Love is a word
devoid of love.
I came back to you defeated;
I've been fighting life's battles
with a sword forged from feeling.

I came back to you .. and laid my anchor
on the sand.
As I washed my face with dew
it seemed you were calling me.

يا صحراء
شعر: غازي عبد الرحمن القصيبي
المملكة العربية السعودية

وطفتُ الكونَ .. لم أعثرْ
على أجدبَ من أرضكْ
على أطهرَ من حبّكْ
أوَ أعنفَ من بُغضِكْ

وعدتُ اليك يا صحراءُ
على وجهي رذاذُ البحرْ
وفي روحي سرابُ بكاءْ
وطيفٌ سابحٌ في السحرْ
ووميضُ ضفيرةٍ شقراءْ
وفي شفتيّ بيتٌ شعرْ
وأغنيةٌ بلا أصداءْ

رجعتُ إليكِ مهموماً
لأني لم أجدْ في الناسِ
مَن يؤمنُ بالنّاسِ
رجعتُ إليكِ محروماً
لأنّ الكونَ أضلاعٌ
بلا قلبِ
لأنّ الحبَّ ألفاظٌ
مجرّدةٌ من الحبّ
رجعتُ إليكِ مهزوماً
لأنّي خضتُ معركةَ الحياةِ
بسيفِ إحساسي

وعدتُ إليكِ .. ألقيتُ مرساتي
على الرملِ
غسلتُ الوجهَ بالطلِّ
كأنّكِ عندها ناديتني

Then you whispered:
"Have you come back to me, my child?"
Yes .. mother .. I came back to you.
A child, forever grieving,
flew to God's countries;
unable to find his nest,
he came back to search for his life in you.

I came back to you, oh desert.
I've thrown away my quiver and ceased wandering.
I dally in your night-web
of mystery,
breathing on the soft winds of the Najd*
the fragrance of Araar*.
In you I live for poetry and moons.

Ghazi al-Qusaibi [al-Gosaibi]
Saudi Arabia

* Najd: Province in Saudi Arabia.
* Araar: A sweetly-scented white flower growing in the Najd.

وهمست في أذني
"رجعتَ إليَّ يا طفلي؟"
أجل .. أمّاه .. عُدتُ إليكِ
طفلًا دائم الحُزنِ
تغرّبَ في بلادِ الله
لم يعثرْ على وكرٍ
وعاد اليومَ يبحثُ فيكِ عن عمرِ

وعُدتُ إليكِ يا صحراءُ
القي جعبةَ التسيارِ
أغازلُ نيلكِ المنسوجَ
مِن أسرارْ
وانشقُ في صبا نجدٍ
طيوبَ عَرارْ
وأحيا فيكِ للأشعارِ والأقمارْ

PALM TREE

He asked "What's a palm tree?" so I replied, "Motherhood and selfless charity,
giving deepest shade from the burning sun, an overflowing source of abundant beauty
with superb patience as barefooted blades crowd in to cut, burn and bury."

He asked "Who at your place slaughters these trees, leaving them dry with a spring near by?
Is there no one among you burning with zeal to stand up and protest publicly?"
"They talk .. we talk .. that's all I can say, but what's the use, no one listens today."

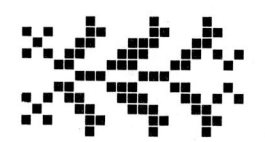

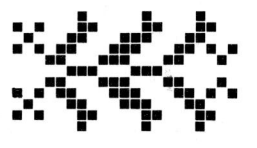

Abd al-Rahman Rafi'
Bahrain

النخل
شعر: عبدالرحمن رفيع
(البحرين)

ويسألني: ما النخلُ؟ قلتُ أمومةٌ ** ويبذلُ وإحسانٌ عظيمٌ بلا مَنِّ
وظلٌّ ظليلٌ في الهجيرِ ومنظرٌ ** تفجّرَ منه منبعٌ فاضَ بالحسنِ
وصبرٌ جميلٌ والمناجلُ كُشِّرَتْ ** لتمطرَها بالقطعِ والحرقِ والدفنِ

ويسألني: من ينبحُ النخلَ عندكم ** ويتركهُ ميتاً في قربهِ النبعُ؟
أما فيكم من يستشيطُ حميّةً ** ليجهرَ بالشكوى فيسمعَ الجمعُ
فقلتُ له: قالوا، وقلنا.. ولم يزلْ ** يقالُ.. وما نفعُ الكلامِ ولا سمعُ

PERPLEXITY

Perplexed, as you've seen, in the city,
like doomed caravans we are lost.
Days in our overcrowded lives have no dimension;
we have only our weeping hearts during sleepless nights
or a quill squeaking across the surface of manuscripts
which become moist with tobacco and sweat.
We are weighed down in a swamp of boredom,
the walls feeding on the bones of stagnant silence.
Our existence ... the humiliation of life in the gutter
can be seen from the forehead of an old man whose hand is trembling,
its veins crying out for bread.
But the exhausted street, like a river, swallows the echo.

Geeli Abd al-Rahman
Sudan

حيرة

شعر: جيلي عبد الرحمن
(السودان)

وحائرونَ ـ مثلما رأيتُ في المدينهْ
وضائعونَ كالقوافلِ المسكينهْ
أيامُنا في زحمةِ الحياةِ لا أبعادْ
سوى نحيبِ القلبِ في السهادْ
وريشةٍ تصرُّ فوقَ كومةِ الورقْ
تبتلُّ بالدخانِ والعرقْ
يثقلُنا ما يثقلُ المستنقعَ الضجرْ
مسكينةٌ تفتّاتْ من عظامِها الجدرْ
حياتُنا... يا ذلةَ الحياةِ في الرصيفْ
على جبينِ شيخٍ يُرعِشُ اليدا
عروقُها تستصرخُ الرغيفْ
والشارعُ المنهوكُ نهرٌ يبلعُ الصدى

TO MY SON OMAR

(Excerpts)

The house is calm but I'm restless,
if your sheet slips, they jump
and consumed with concern, I rush
I'm alone .. with no friend .. except you,

When morning comes .. your toys
for you and I share a world
We are alone with God,
Oh flower of my life! My lily,
fragrant, white and pure.

my eyes are glued to your bed,
right out of my head
to listen and watch over you.
my night and my companion.

are ready with picture books;
filled with fun and lessons.
this is written .. by destiny.
in my hands you're growing up,
Green-leafed basil of spring.

Abd al-Mun'im al-Rifa'i
Jordan

إلى ولدي عمر
شِعر: عبدالمنعم الرفاعي
الأردن

مُقتطفات

سكنَ المبيتُ سوى مؤرقةٍ :: قد شدَّها لسريرك النظرُ
إن زلَّ عنك غطاؤك انخلعَتْ :: عيني… وقمتُ إليك أبتدرُ
أحنو عليك… وكلُّ جارحةٍ :: تخنو معي… والسمعُ والبصرُ
أصبحتُ وحدي… لا يشاركُني :: خلٌّ… وأنتَ الليلُ والسمرُ

طلعَ الصباحُ… فهذهِ لعبٌ :: صفَفتُ إليك… وهذه صورُ
وأنا وأنتَ… كأنَّ عالمَنا :: لهوٌ… وكلُّ بقائهِ عِبَرُ
في وحدةِ اللهِ ثالثُها :: كتبتُ… وخطَّ سطورَها القدرُ
يا زهرةَ الأيام! زنبقتي :: في راحتي اليومَ تزدهرُ
فوّاحةً… بيضاءَ… صافيةً :: ريحانةً أوراقُها خضرُ

READ THEM
– PAPERS OF A DEAD MAN –

Here's my room .. oblivion's corroded and silence has grown old.
Enter with candles, this room's a lair carved from the breast of darkness.
Walk very slowly or you may frighten the dust and spiders!
Near my broken cup .. a bundle of papers; between covers a lifetime's scattered.
Take them .. they contain your youth and the beauty which caused me to suffer.
Read them, don't deny me immortality .. Publish them, don't let me die.

Umar Abu Rishah
Syria

إقرأيها

«أوراق ميت» شعر: عمر أبو ديش
(سوريا)

إنّها حجرتي .. لقد صدى النسيان فيها .. وشاخ فيها السكوتُ
ادخلي بالشموع .. فهي من الظلمة وكرٌ في صدرها منحوتُ
وانقلي الخطو بائتئادٍ فقد يحفل منك الغار والعنكبوتُ!
عند كأسي المكسور .. حزمةُ أوراقٍ وعمري في دفتيها شتيتُ
إحمليها .. ماضيَ شبابك فيها .. والفنون الذي عليه شقيتُ
إقرأيها .. لا تحجبي الخلد عنّي .. إنشريها .. لا تتركيني أموتُ

CLOUDS WITHOUT RAIN

With our burden of misery, we move
towards the gates of hope.
We pray and pray for rain
where we used to sow love
to be nurtured by the moon.
The sun darkens,
yet still the eyes of heaven shed no tears.
Thundering clouds descend upon us
without rain.
Is this a time of despair, is this
an age being born out of the wombs of graves?
Oh deliver us from the curse.
Oh stone age.

Adib Sa'b
Lebanon

سحب من غير ماء

شعر: أديب صعب

(لبنان)

حاملين البؤس، نمضي
نحو أبواب الرجاء
ونصلّي ونصلّي للمطر
حيث كنّا نغرس الحب
ويسقيه القمر
غيران الشمس تسود
ولا تدمع مع غيم للسماء
ثم تنهال علينا
سحب راعدة من غير ماء
أترى هذا أوان اليأس
هذا زمن يولد من بطن الحفر؟
آه! اخلصنا من اللعنة
يا عصر الحجر

CITY OF HUMAN BEINGS

Night in my city is red,
the red of smoke and dust.
All who live here
are consumed with hate for one another.
This city humiliates its builders.

Its domes are merely ornamental.
It is a sad city.
Every virgin
sleeps beside her doorway
watching for dawn which never breaks;
without dawn, this is a playground for apes.

Day is as dark as night,
even the stars are black.
No singing can be heard or poetry;
it is like a graveyard dug by rogues.

My city's like a statue,
painted and finely moulded, but lifeless.
Even the women live without hope.
Money in my city, money,
sells .. buys .. hires men.
Everything in my city has a price,
sex, children, houses.
No rain falls from the clouds over my city
and its earth is rock.
Its people .. who are its people?
Human beings!

مدينة ناسها بشر
شعر : علي السبتي
(الكويت)

الليلُ في مدينتي أحمرْ
لكنّهُ من الدخانِ والغبارِ أحمرْ
وكلُّ مَنْ فيها
يكرهُ مَنْ فيها
لأنهاتْ تذلُّ بانيها

قبابها قد بُنيتْ للزينهْ
فهي مدينةٌ حزينهْ
وكلُّ عذراءَ بها
تنامُ عندَ بابها
تنظرُ الصباحَ .. والصباحُ لا يعودْ
لأنّه من دونهِ ملاعبُ القرودْ

نهارها كليلها ظُلمهْ
حتى النجومُ فيها عتمهْ
ولا «ليالي» إنْ أصختْ السمع لا موّالْ
كأنها مقبرةٌ حفّارها مُحتالْ

مدينتي كأنها تمثالْ
ملوّنٌ مُزركشٌ لكنّه تمثالْ
حتى النساءُ في مدينتي بلا آمالْ
المالُ في مدينتي، المالْ
يبيعُ .. يشتري .. يستأجرُ الرجالْ
فكلُّ شئٍ في مدينتي له ثمنْ
الجنسُ والأطفالُ والسكنْ
مدينتي غيومها بلا مطرْ
وأرضها حجرْ
وناسها .. مَنْ ناسها؟
بشرْ!

I would like, oh my city, to gather your rocks
and command destiny
to wash away from this city I love,
all these human beings.

Oh my city! When shall I see you
teeming with real people?

Ali al-Sab'ti
Kuwait

اودُّ يا مَدينَتي لوَ أجمـع الحجَرْ
وآمـرُ القـدَرْ
فَيغسلُ المَدينة التي أحبُّها
من البشَـــرْ

مَدِينَـتي! متىٰ أراكِ تزدَهـين
بِالبَشَــرْ؟

EULOGY FOR AN INSIGNIFICANT MAN

He died .. the way he'd lived,
pitiful and trodden upon
like rubble in a graveyard.
His sallow death was sudden,
expected, unexpected,
death upon death.
He had no family and no friends
for he'd never shared
the joys of childhood
so no one remained close during his youth.
He was always alone, bleeding like a passing rain-cloud,
as commonplace as any fly.
I knew him.
As I landed each morning in the lake of human suffering, I would see him,
while collecting in my skin bag
a few dust-edged crumbs,
scattered by boys to dogs and fowls.
Whenever I rejected a too filthy crust,
he would seize it, dust it on his sleeve, kiss it and swallow it, saying:
"In a world like this
insignificant men are blind to dirt in food and drink."
You ask, was he my friend?
How can there be friendship between travellers?
Why then, when I heard of his death,
did I weep?
Why did a sense of desolation remain with me for two nights?
Why do I write this eulogy?

Salah Abd al-Sabur
Egypt

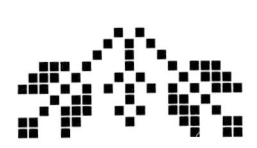

مرثية رجل تافه
شعر: صلاح عبد الصبور
(مصر)

مضت حياته.. كما مضت
ذليلةً موطأةْ
كأنها تراب مقبرْ
وكان موت الغريب باهتاً مباغتاً
منتظراً مفاجئاً
الميتة المكررهْ
كان بلا أهل بلا أصحاب
فلم يشارك صاحباً
حين الصبا لهو الصبا
ليحفظ الوداد في الشباب
كان وحيداً نازفاً كعابر السحاب
وشائعاً كما الذباب
وكنتُ أعرفهْ
أراه كلما رسا بي الصباح في بحيرة العذاب
أجمع في الجراب
بضع لقيمات تناثرتْ على شطوطها التراب
ألقى بها الصبيان للدجاج والكلاب
وكنت إن تركت لقمة أنفت أن ألمها
يلقطها، يمسحها في كفه، يسوسها، يأكلها
في عالم كعالم الذي نعيش فيه
تغشى عيون التافهين عن وساخة الطعام والشراب
وتسألوني.. أكان صاحبي؟
وكيف صحبة تقوم بين راحلين؟
إذن لماذا حينما نمى الناعي إليّ نعيهْ
بكيتهْ
وزارني حزني الغريب لليلتين
ثم رثيته؟

I TOLD YOU

I told you I listened to the poetry
of the sea; I listened
to the bell which rests in every shell.
I told you I sang
at the devil's wedding .. at the feast of legends.
I told you I could see
through the rain of history .. and the glow of distance,
a genie and a dwelling place.
Because I drift into my own dreams,
I told you I saw everything
from my very first step into the distance.

Ali Ahmad Sa'id ('Adonis')
Syria

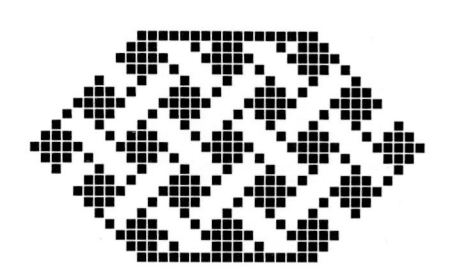

قلتُ لكم
شعر: أدونيس
(سوريا)

قلتُ لكمُ أصغيتُ للبحارِ
تقرألي أشعارها، أصغيتْ
للجرسِ النائمِ في المحارِ
قلتُ لكمُ غنّيتُ
في عرسِ الشيطانِ.. في وليمةِ الخُرافهْ
قلتُ لكمُ رأيتُ
في مطرِ التاريخِ.. في توهّجِ المسافهْ
حنّيةً وبيتْ
لأنّني أبحرُ في عيني
قلتُ لكمُ رأيتُ كلّ شيءْ
في الخطوةِ الأولى من المسافهْ

FEMININE AND MASCULINE

You ask about long hair
and about unisex clothes,
since females dress like males,
Both parade in jeans
crosses wink on their chests,
as they roam the streets with disdain,
It's simple, this is equality,
going far beyond all reason,
if this craziness increases,
and men sprout luscious breasts.
in our era of trips to the moon,
and how it's the fashion for men
with signs of gender gone;
who can tell them apart?
and shoes with very high heels,
belts are pulled tightly in
their make-up overdone.
as you see it's a rotten idea,
for reversed sexes are here.
women may soon sprout beards
Indeed it's not impossible:
there's sure to be one sex soon.

Muhammad al-Akhdar al-Sa'ihi
Algeria

التأنيث والتذكير
شعر: محمد الأخضر السائحي
(الجزائر)

تسألني عن موضة الشعور ### وكيف صارت صفة الذكور
وعن لباس وحّد الاثنين ### وطار بالمعنى من الجنسين
فأصبح التأنيث كالتذكير ### وأشكل الأمر على التفسير
كلاهما يخطر في السروال ### ويلبس النعل بكعب عالِ
يعلّق الصليب فوق الصدر ### ويضغط الحزام حول الخصر
يفرط في التزيين والتزويق ### وينبذ الحياء في الطريق
الأمر سهل إنه التساوي ### وهو كما ترى من المساوي
قد جاوز الحدّ من الإسراف ### وعاد بالوضع إلى الخلاف
وربما زاد من الجنون ### فعادت النساء بالذقون
وثارت النهود في الرجال ### فليس هذا الأمر بالمحال
فنحن في عهد الصعود للقمر ### لا فرق فيه بين أنثى أو ذكر

PERHAPS

Perhaps there are others as lovely as you.
But,
the pious beauty of your mouth is sweeter.
Perhaps seductive glances
conquer, but,
my darling sparrow
you are more alluring by far.
Perhaps I loved before,
but you
– with your quivering eyelashes –
are more precious,
a thousand times more precious.

Ahmad Salih al-Salih
Saudi Arabia

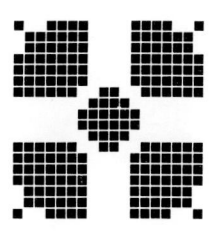

ربّما

شعر: أحمد صالح الصالح
(المملكة العربيّة السعوديّة)

ربّما غيرك حلوات
ولكن
خشوع الحسن في ثغرك أحلى
ربّما الإغراء في الأعين
يجتاح ولكنّك
يا عصفورتي
عيناك في الإغراء أقوى
ربّما أحببتُ
لكنّك
يا راعشة الأهداب
أغلى
ألف أغلى

TO THE FATHOMLESS DEPTHS, TAKE ME

(Excerpts)

Where are you going? Silence is killing me,
give me your hands .. and hold mine,
to the fathomless depths, take me.
Don't destroy the dream,
between your vision and this dream,
my soul is softly weeping.
Don't destroy Eid in the eye of a child
who jumps over time to meet you – her Eid.*

Come, let me teach your eyes
how to challenge.
You are still on the shore,
at the very beginning of passion.
Give me your hands and hold mine.
To the fathomless depths, take me.

My heart is those depths.

'Ru'a Salim'
United Arab Emirates

* Eid Al Fitr is the first day of Shawwal following Ramadhan. The breaking of the holy fast, called the lesser feast, is a time of celebration.

Eid Al Adha. These are the days of festivities concluding the pilgrimage. Muslims, whether in Mecca or at home, observe this day and participate in the distribution of food. Muslims require no invitation to call on one another at this time. Special prayers are always offered during the Eids after sunrise.

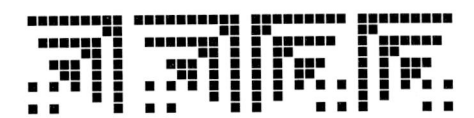

إلى القاع خذني
شعر: رؤى سالم
مقتطفات (الإمارات العربية المتحدة)

إلى أين ترحل .. يقتلني الصمتُ
هاتِ يديكَ .. وخُذ بيدي
إلى القاع خذني
ولا تقتل الحلمَ
ما بين عينيك والحلمِ
تقطر أنداءُ روحي
ولا تقتل العيدَ في عينِ طفلٍ
يوثّبُ هذا الزمانَ ليلقاك عيداً

تعالَ .. أعلّم عينيك
كيف يكون التحدّي
فما زلتَ في شاطئ البدءِ
في أوّل العشقِ
هاتِ يديكَ وخُذ بيدي
إلى القاع خذني

فقلبي هو القاعُ

HER BIRTHDAY

Your birthday: dawn's first light   fills the world with radiance.
    Birds drunk with the wind
    soar on wings of song.

Your birthday: day breaks,   everywhere flowers are preening
    as the smiling brilliance of the world
    lights up my horizons.

Is it you or April,   filling the world with magic?
    Our lives are overflowing
    with the singing fragrance of gardens.

You are my shade;   without you life would be a mirage.
    Your smile is so enchanting
    I shall smile for ever.

You're the perfume of dreams,   a celebration of light and music.
    Of all God's poems in the universe,
    you are the dearest and most subtle.

Your exquisite birthday   pours love into my veins
    so my poems are soaked in magic
    like the myths of ancient Greece.

Nurradin Sammud
Tunisia

عيدُ ميلادِها

شعر : نور الدين صمّود

تونس،

عيدُ ميلادِكِ انبثاقُ شُعاعٍ   يملأُ الكونَ بالسّنى اللمّاعِ
فتهبُّ الطيورُ هيمي نشاوى
وتعمُّ الوجودَ بالإيقاعِ

عيدُ ميلادكِ انبثاقةُ فجرٍ   وزهورٌ تفتّرُ في كلّ ثغرِ
كابتساماتِ عالمٍ عبقريٍّ
غمرتْ بالضياءِ آفاقَ عمري

أنتِ أقبلتِ .. أم ترى نيسانُ   يملأُ الكونَ سحرُهُ الفتّانُ
فيفيضُ الوجودُ سحراً وعطراً
وتضوعُ الزهورُ والألحانُ

أنتِ ظلٌّ لو لم تكوني بعمري   كان عمري مثلَ السرابِ بقفرِ
ومذا فترّةٍ تُخرِكَ الحلوِ لاحت
بسمةٌ سرمديةٌ فوقَ ثغري

أنتِ يا نفحةَ الشذى والأماني   يا انبثاقَ الأضواءِ والألحانِ
أنتِ أغلى قصائدِ الكونِ معنىً
صاغَها اللهُ من أرقِّ المعاني

عيدُ ميلادكِ الرقيقُ الرفيقُ   سكبَ العطرَ والهوى في عروقي
فسرى في قصائدي طيفُ سحرٍ
كأساطيرِ شاعرٍ إغريقي

IF THE CITY WISHED

City of stars,
city sinking into gloom.
People walking on footpaths
and street-crossings
are shadowed by claws of eagles;
they are choking
as though in their death-throes.
The days of their lives
recede into the past
and their eyes are dull
as though veiled by mist.

City of stars,
city without dreams.
City wandering,
as though in a wave not from the sea –
a sterile wave without shells.
The spreading shadows are toneless,
even scents have vanished. Aspirations
are blazing with the garbage.
Time, consuming the misery
of the city
grows heavy
and stops.
Smoke blurs
while eddies of heat
lash faces.
Doors of the city are opened to strangers.

إذا تشاء المدينة
شعر: محمد السرغيني
(المغرب)

مدينةُ النجومْ
مدينةٌ تغوصُ في الوجومْ
والناسُ في دروبها
في ملتقى سهوبها
تظلهم مخالبُ العقابْ
ويسعلون
كأنهم في ظلمة احتضارْ
ومن وراء عمرهم
ينحسرُ النهارْ
وتنطفي أعينهم
كأنها ضبابْ

مدينةُ النجومْ
مدينةٌ بلا رؤى
مدينةٌ نَهِمْ
في موجةٍ لا تنتمي إلى البحارْ
في موجةٍ عقيمةٍ بلا محارْ
الظلُ من أغصانها لا لونَ له
والعطرُ ماتْ . شوقها
على سعيرِ مزبلهْ
وكلما توقّف الزمنْ
يَنُوءُ تحت عبئها
يعبُ ما في فيئها
من الشجنْ
يمسخها الدخانْ
ويصفعُ اللهيبْ
بسوطه الوجوهْ
فتفتحُ المدينةُ الأبوابَ للغريبْ

Time diminishes
and the place fades.

City of despair,
city without care.
If it wished the dumb would shout,
dawn would break everywhere
and darkness be blown out.

Muhammad al-Sarghini
Morocco

فيضولُ الزمانْ
ويشحبُ المكانْ

مدينةُ الوجومْ
مدينةٌ بلا همومْ
إذا تشاءُ ينطقُ الخرسْ
فيورقُ السكونُ في ربوعِها
وينطفي الغلسْ

IN THE GARDEN

My daughter's playing with her dog in the garden,
her mother's gone out,　　　　now's her chance to be free.
She runs across lawns breaking every decree;
the branch she bends on an elegant tree
is leafy one moment, a bare swing the next.
She waters so generously,　　dry plants are drowning,
you'd think she's quenching　fire with fire.
This sister of roses　　　　　attacks the roses,
now she's teasing a canary,　half-choked, it's cheeping.
Her dog, who guards her,　　swallows saliva,
fearing a smack for his reckless friend
and I, in my chair,　　　　　am the happiest of men;
as I pretend not to notice,　but watch every antic.
Behind my glasses　　　　　there's a grateful tear,
for a lover's joy　　　　　　at his darling's laughter
and for dreams that are　　reality here.
My tears wash away　　　　past sins of passion;
my tears implore the harsh heart of time
to transform my whole life　into hours in the garden.

George Saydah
Syria. Latin America.

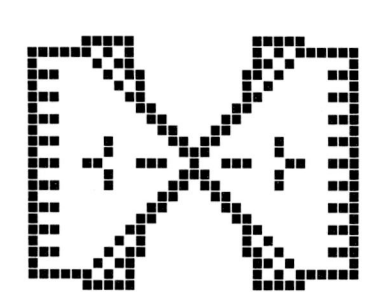

في الحديقة

شعر: جورج صبيح
(المهجر)

ابنتي مع كلبها تلعبُ   في رحب الحديقه
أمّها غابت فهذي   فرصة البنت الطليقه
خالفت في دعسها العشبَ المراسمَ الوثيقه
ولوت أعناق أغصان الشجيرات الأنيقه
مورقات، أصبحت أرجوحة اللهو الخليقه
رشرشتها بسخاءٍ   ترك العطشى غريقه
من رآها ظنها   تطفئ بالنار حريقه
ربّ وردٍ هاجمته   وهي للورد شقيقه
وكنارٍ داعبته   خنق الضغط شهيقه
كلبها المسؤول عنها   قلق يبلع ريقه
خائف عاقبة الطيش على ردف الرفيقه
وأنا في مقعدي   أسعدُ حيٍّ في الخليقه
أتغاضى، وعيوني   لم تفارقها دقيقه
خلف منظاري توارت   دمعة الشكر الرقيقه
دمعة العاشق لا يروعه   ضحك العشيقه
دمعة أفزعت الأحلام   في جفن الحقيقه
دمعة تغسل أوزار   الصبابات العتيقه
دمعة تستعطف الدهر.. وتستبقيك صفيقه
ليته يجمع عمري   في سويعات الحديقه

THE VACATION

Grumbling, he slapped one hand on his wretched gut
and asked: "What were you suggesting?"
She unzipped the back of her dress
"I was going to say,
but the news,
look,
there's beautiful Beirut.
What a pity."
She leaned towards him:
"We'll spend the summer
in New York .. London's
crowded with Arabs and terrorists.
The Irish have lost their heads
and have you forgotten about
the recent Falklands war?"

Habib al-Sayegh
United Arab Emirates

عُطلة
شعر: حبيب الصائغ
(الإمارات العربية المتحدة)

متأفّفاً، وضع اليد اليمنى على الكرش الرجيم
وقال: ماذا كنتِ تقترحين؟
حكّت ظهرها
قالت: سأمضي في الكلام
ولكن الأخبار
أنظر
تلك بيروت الجميلة
يا خساره
ثم مالت نحوه
قالت: سنقضي صيف هذا العام
في نيويورك.. لندن أصبحت
مكتظّة عرباً وإرهاباً
فإيرلندا تمادت في الجنون
وإن نسيتُ فهل ستنسى
حرب فوكلاند الأخيره؟

SOUND

A dumb man
and woman meet.
He smiles .. The woman smiles.
He beckons .. She nods.
He gets up .. She follows.
He walks .. She walks by his side
until they reach the end of the world.
Confused, the man stops,
wondering:
Isn't it time she realised I'm dumb?
While the woman standing beside him
is also wondering:
Isn't it time he realised I'm dumb?

Yusuf al-Sayegh
Iraq

صوتٌ
شعر: يوسف الصائغ
(العراق)

رجلٌ أخرسْ
وامرأةٌ خرساءْ
يلتقيانْ
يبتسمْ .. تبتسمُ المرأةْ
يومئُ .. تومئُ
ينهضُ .. تتبعهُ
يمشي .. تمشي معهُ
حتى يصلا آخرَ هذي الدنيا
يقفُ الرجلُ الأخرسُ مرتبكاً
يتساءلُ:
ما آنَ لها أن تفهمَ أني رجلٌ أخرسْ؟
في حينِ تظلُّ المرأةُ واقفةً قربهُ
تتساءلُ:
ما آنَ له أن يفهمَ أني امرأةٌ خرساءْ؟

BURNING

Even when I melt your stone body in my fire
and dash away snow from your hands; there remain between your eyes and mine
vast wastes of snow exhausting the night traveller,
as though you're watching me from distant nebulae and moons.
Although we are together, it seems we're waiting to meet;
but waiting for love is a meeting .. where shall we meet?
Torn is your naked body.
Torn under the dome of night are your breasts by my nails.
Torn by the intensity of my passion is everything .. except those veils
concealing in you all that I most desire.
As if your blood which I drink is salt, I remain thirsty
when I try to quench my thirst. Where is your love .. where is your bare heart?
I bolt the door of night against it .. then I embrace the door,
kissing in it my shadow, my memories and some of my secrets.
I search for you within my fire
but I do not find you, I do not find your ashes in the blazing flame.
I will throw myself into its flame with all that is absent
and present.
I want you .. kill me so I may feel you.
Kill the stone
with a surge of blood .. with fire from you
and burn without fire.

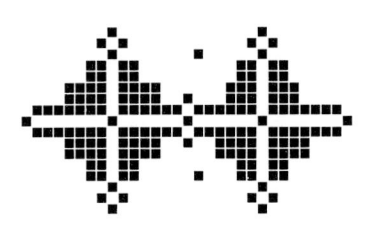

Badr Shakir al-Sayyab
Iraq

إحتراق

شعر : بدر شاكر السيّاب
(العراق)

وحتّى حين أصهر جسمك الحجري في ناري
وأنزع من يديك الثلج، تبقى بين عينينا
صحارى من ثلوج تنهك الساري
كأنك تنظرين إليّ من سُدمٍ وأقمارْ
كأنا، منذُ كنّا، في إنتظار ما تلاقينا
ولكنّ انتظار الحبّ لقيا .. أين لقيانا
تمزّق جسمك العاري
تمزّق تحت سقف الليل نهدُكِ بين أظفاري
تمزّق من لهيبي كلّ شيء .. غير أستارٍ
تحجّب فيك ما أهواه
كأنّي أشربُ الدّم فيك ملحًا، ظلَّ عطشانا
من استسقاه .. أين هواك؟ أين فؤادك العاري
أسُدُّ عليه باب الليل .. ثمّ أعانقُ البابا
فألثم فيه ظلّي، ذكرياتي، بعض أسراري
وأبحثُ عنك في ناري
فلا ألقاك – لا ألفى رمادكِ في اللظى الواري
سأقذف كلّ نفسي في لظاها، كلّ ما غابا
وما حضرا
أريدك .. فاقتليني كي أحسّكِ
واقتلي المجرّا
بفيض دمٍ .. بنارٍ منكِ
واحترقي بلا نارِ.

THE CUP

I've wrung my heart into a cup of love
"Wine doesn't quench our thirst", they said.
even the poor deny our richness of spirit,
I dissolved my heart in a cup of love
"Here's justice, so drink from this cup", I said,
They turned away from my cup, grumbling,
I dissolved my heart in a cup of love
"Here's comfort for your hearts", I urged,
"Blood can't unfasten chains", they cried,
I dissolved my heart in a cup of love
"This is true light, so drink", I said,
Shaking their heads in scorn, they sighed,
I dissolved my heart in a cup of love
"Here's true nobility, so drink
"You insult our ancestors' pride", they hissed,
I dissolved my heart in a cup of love
"This is true love, so drink", I said,
if love does not inflame your hearts,
I still wandered the world with my wine,
when despair overcame me, I chose solitude,
I dissolved my heart in a cup of love
I saw my heart in my cup smiling,
so I raised my cup to my lips and drank

and raised it to the lips of the poor.
I muttered, "Alas we're miserable poets,
but what nourishment do we provide for the poor?"
and raised it to the lips of rulers.
"so you may listen to the words of the weak."
"Your cup's prohibited to leaders."
and raised it to the lips of prisoners.
"my blood's for the wretched innocent."
"give us new laws so we may be free."
and raised it to the lips of the wise.
"for your views require enlightenment."
"Your light's a lure for the ignorant."
and raised it to the lips of princes.
and proceed with my cup to other nobles."
"and all men who are born noble."
and raised it to the lips of poets.
"or your pawned garments may be lost for ever;" *
you're hideous .. with a thousand garments."
while people jeered at my constancy;
to search once more for remnants of hope.
to drink it mixed with my own tears,
in humble pride-touched innocence,
and it's still filled with the water of love.

Ilyas Abu Shabakah
Lebanon

* Garments is used here to mean poems.

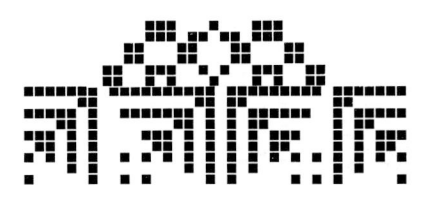

الإناء
شعر: إلياس أبو شبكة
(لبنان)

عصرتُ فؤادي في إناءٍ من الهوى   وأدنيتهُ من مرشفِ الفقراء
فقالوا خمورٌ ما تبرّدُ غلّةً   فمتمتمتُ: واهًا أكبدَ الشعراء
أينكرُ حتّى البؤسُ ما فيكَ من غنًى   وأيُّ غذاءٍ أنت للبؤساء؟
وذوّبتُ قلبي في إناءٍ من الهوى   وأدنيتهُ من مرشفِ الرؤساء
وقلتُ لهم هذا هو العدلُ فاشربوا   لعلّكم تصغونَ للضعفاء
فمالوا جميعًا عن إنائي وغمغموا   إناؤكَ محظورٌ على الزعماء
وذوّبتُ قلبي في إناءٍ من الهوى   وأدنيتهُ من مرشفِ السجناء
وقلتُ لهم هذا عزاءٌ قلوبكم   فللأبرياءِ التاعسينَ دمائي
فقالوا دماءٌ ما تحلُّ قيودنا   فهاتِ قوانينًا لغيرِ قضاء
وذوّبتُ قلبي في إناءٍ من الهوى   وأدنيتهُ من مرشفِ الحكماء
وقلتُ لهم هذا هو النورُ فاشربوا   فأراؤكم في حاجةٍ لضياء
فقالوا وقد هزّوا الرؤوسَ شماتةً   ضياؤكَ هذا خدعةٌ للجهلاء
فذوّبتُ قلبي في إناءٍ من الهوى   وأدنيتهُ من مرشفِ الأمراء
وقلتُ لهم هذا هو النبلُ فاشربوا   وطوفوا بأقداحي على النبلاء
فقالوا أتحقيرٌ لطغراءِ جدّنا   وما تنسلُ الأصلابُ من شُرَفاء؟
وذوّبتُ قلبي في إناءٍ من الهوى   وأدنيتهُ من مرشفِ الشعراء
وقلتُ لهم هذا هو الحبُّ فاشربوا   فأزياؤكم مرهونةٌ لفناء
إذا الحبُّ لم يضرم لهيبَ قلوبكم   بشعركمُ... ولو جئتم بألف رداء
ومازلتُ في الدنيا أطوفُ بخمرتي   وحولي شعبٌ هازئٌ بوفائي
إلى أن دهاني اليأسُ فاخترتُ عزلةً   أفتّشُ فيها عن حطامِ رجائي
وذوّبتُ خمري في إناءٍ من الهوى   لأشربها ممزوجةً ببكائي
فشاهدتُ قلبي في إنائي ضاحكًا   به دعةُ عذراءَ في خلاء
فأدنيتهُ من مرشفي... وشربتهُ   وما زال ماءُ الحبِّ ملءَ إنائي

THE POET'S HOUSE

(Excerpts)

A disintegrating house,
like a discarded hag,
Teeming with spiders and scorpions,
nails hammered into walls,
How many mice are flying,
How strange they do not fear
quite beyond repair,
without finery or jewels.
the quilts are spun from dust;
drop out onto floors.
as flies switch humming tones?
collapsing ceilings and doors.

Ahmad al-Sharif
Libya

دَارُ الأديبِ
شِعرُ: أحمد الشارفُ
(ليبيا)

مُقتطفات

دَارٌ لَقَدْ بَلِيَتْ فَلَا تَنْظيمُها :: يَحلُو... وَلَا كَلٌّ وَلَا أَسْتَارُ

كَدَميمَةٍ شَمْطاءَ لَيْسَ يَزينُها :: حُلَىً وَلَا حَلَلٌ وَلَا أَزْرارُ

فيها العَقارِبُ والعَناكِبُ جَمَّةٌ :: ومِنَ التُّرابِ على الفِراشِ غُبارُ

إنْ دُقَّ مِسْمارٌ على جَنَباتِها :: يَنقَضُّ منهُ ويَسقُطُ المِسْمارُ

كَمْ فَأْرَةٍ طارَتْ بها وذُبابَةٍ :: طَنَّتْ وكَمْ لِطَنينِها أدوارُ

عَجَبًا بها لَمْ تَخْشَ مِنْ سَقْفٍ بها :: يَهوي ومِنْ جُدُرٍ بها تَنهارُ

RAIN

Perhaps you don't remember,
perhaps you do,
when we walked together in the echo of night,
    while rain,
blue as the taste of the sky,
    was falling
        into my blood and into the heart of trees.
You asked: "Where are you taking me?"
I answered: "To be led swiftly
By that path which lets our surging feelings erupt and sing in their own wild way.
Exquisite, oh companion of my soul, is this way,
    leading only to
      love."
We walked.
Your fingers like fire
in my hand. Warm rain
falling into rivulets on the friendly road,
protected us
like its own children, from the cold.
My hand was aching
with the heat of my desire.
Rain possessed us
and planeted us up in the clouds as stars to watch our dreams reflected in the river.
We walked,
raindrops whirling to our feet.
This was the rising dawn of our adolescence.

مطر
شعر: علي الشرقاوي
(البحرين)

ربّما أنتِ لا تذكرين
ربّما تذكرين
حين سرنا معاً في صدى الليل
كان المطر
أزرقاً مثل طعم المسا
هابطاً
في دمي وفؤاد الشجر
قلتِ: أين ستأخذني؟
قلتُ: نترك أقدامنا
لجموح المشاعر تصهل فوق البراكين
حلو رفيقة روحي الطريق الذي
لا يقود سوى
للهوى.

مشينا
أصابعكِ في يدي
مثلما النآر، كان المطر
يتساقط دفئاً على خصلات الطريق الصديق
يدثّرنا
مثل أطفال الخارجين إلى البرد
صادفت وجدي حريقاً
وأنتِ يدي
يرتدينا المطر
ويكوكبنا في الغيوم نجوماً نرى حلمها في النهر
مشينا
تدحرج فوق دمينا المطر
تسلق فينا الصباح المراهق

Rain was
   titillating us as fragrant nectar lures bees,
      or burning desire draws one on.
We were the rebellious dawn.
Rain was
   falling across the horizon of our vision,
      through the flaming heat of noon
         into our sighing hearts.
Rain was.
Perhaps you remember,
perhaps.
Ah, but I
   shall always remember.

Ali al-Sharqawi
Bahrain

كانَ المطرْ
يعذّبنا كالرحيق يهيمُ برائحة النحل
أو كالحريق المهاجم عبرَ الضلوع
وكنّا الطلوعَ المشاكس

كانَ المطرْ
يتساقطُ في أفقِ العين
في جذوةِ الظهر
في شهقةِ القلب

كانَ المطرْ
ربّما تذكرين.
ربّما.
آه. لكنّني
سوف أذكرْ.

THE SAD STAR

Let him finish, he hasn't said all he has to say;
don't withdraw your hands from his.
We don't live twice
yet we die every day.
My friend isn't asking for the moon,
he only wants to inscribe your name on his ship
as an amulet against the wind
and a star to guide him.
My friend doesn't seek a remedy for wounds
for his wound is without remedy.
His only consolation is to sing a little longer
and to see heaven
shining in the depths of your eyes.
My friend says
that during his lifetime he has wept only twice;
once when he was born
and once upon parting.
Like other emigrants, my friend's
horse is grief and his star is sadness.
So will you allow his ship
to pass, to rest in the harbour of your eyes;
to sleep for a moment within the cloak of your affection,
for my friend is without affection?
He has lived without your eyes for years.
If you deny him this glimpse of your eyes
and he drifts away like any emigrant;
if he dies in the shadow of a cypress, he will leave a will
written in tears;
for in his will
there would be only one request –
to pay a short visit to his lonely grave.

Muhammad Ibrahim Abu Sinnah
Egypt

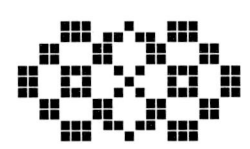

النجم الحزين
شعر: محمد إبراهيم أبو سنة
(مصر)

دعيهِ يكملُ الحديثَ لم يقلْ جميعَ ما لديهْ
لا تَسْحبي يديكِ من يديهْ
فنحنُ لا نعيشُ مرّتين
وإنّما نموتُ كلَّ يومِ
وصاحبي لا يطلبُ القمرْ
يكفيهِ أن يعلّقَ اسمَكِ الجميلَ في سفينةْ
تعويذةً من الرياحْ
ونجمةً أمامَ رحلتهْ
وصاحبي لا يطلبُ الدواءَ للجراحْ
فجرحُهُ بلا دواءْ
عزاؤهُ الوحيدُ أن يُطيلَ في الغناءْ
وأن يرى السماءْ
تضيءُ في عيونكِ الفساحْ
يقولُ صاحبي:
لم يبكِ طيلةَ الحياةِ غيرَ مرّتين
فمرّةً لدى ميلادِهْ
ومرّةً لدى الفراقْ
وصاحبي كأيّ واحدٍ من المهاجرين
جوادُهُ الأسى ونجمُهُ حزينْ
فهل تُراكِ تسمحين للسفينْ
بأن تمرَّ تستريحَ في مرافئ العيونْ
بأن تنامَ لحظةً في معطفِ الحنينْ
فصاحبي بلا حنينْ
يحيا بلا عينيكِ من سنينْ
فإنْ أبيتِ أن تزورَهذه العيونْ
وإن مضى كأيّ واحدٍ من المهاجرين
وماتَ تحتَ سروٍ مخلّفاً وصيّةً
مكتوبةً بدمعتهْ
فليسَ في وصيّتهْ
سوى رجائهِ الوحيدْ
زيارةً قصيرةً لقبرِهِ الوحيدْ.

MOZNAH
ON THE DEATH OF THE POET'S TWENTY-ONE YEAR OLD DAUGHTER

I see you .. when I'm asleep or awake, far away and close to me.
I see you on our cushions and mats; you're there on every path I take.
I see you with your aura of virtue, charming whether you smile or frown.
I see you coming back to me in a mirage or an echoing sound.
I see you, longing for you, in the air and in the water I sip from my cup.
I see you glowing in my mind and in my heart with haloed grace.
I see you - perhaps through you, myself - in the abyss of that uncharted place.
I see you, may God watch over you, immortality of joy and fragrance.*
I see you darling, as you would wait at windows when I came home late.
I see you whichever way I turn, east, west, north and south.

Over you and over your grave may winds carry weeping clouds*
so heavy showers, laden with musk, fall amidst this tearing sound.*
I see rain over every horizon ringing down across the ground
of your resting-place Moznah, my heart is heavy with the sorrow in every heart.

Husain Sirhan
Saudi Arabia

* Favoured form of exaggeration in Arabic.
* It is traditional to pray for rain to fall over the grave of a loved one.
* Among Arab women it is the custom to tear their clothes when somebody dies.

مُزنة

شعر: حسين سرحان
(المملكة العربية السعودية)

أراكِ.. أراكِ.. في نومي وصَحوي — وفي بُعدٍ وفي قُربٍ قَريبِ
أراكِ، على النمارقِ والحَشايا — أراكِ عليَّ آخذةً دُروبي
أراكِ، كثيرَ ما يُبهي محيّاً — على استضحاكهِ وعلى القُطوبِ
أراكِ، على مدى طرفٍ بعيدٍ — أراكِ على صدى صوتٍ مُجيبِ
أراكِ، مع الهواءِ، مع الأماني — مع الماءِ الذي أحسو بكوبي
أراكِ، ملأتِ أخيلتي وقلبي — وأحلامي بكلِّ سنىً حبيبِ
أراكِ، وربّما أبصرتُ نفسي — خلالكِ عبرَ أوديةِ الغيوبِ
أراكِ ـ رأتكِ عينُ اللهِ ـ خُلداً — تضوَّعَ بالمناهجِ والطيوبِ
أراكِ، على النوافذِ في ارتقابي — إذا استنبطاتُ أوبي من ذَهوبي
أراكِ، بكلِّ مُتّجَهٍ.. بشرقٍ — وغربٍ في شمالٍ أو جنوبِ

عليكِ، على ضريحكِ كلُّ مُزنٍ — تهبُّ به الرياحُ مع الهبوبِ
تمجُّ الغيثَ في مسكٍ شتيتٍ — لهُ أرَجٌ.. كمَنبقِ الجيوبِ
أراهُ إذا استطارَ بكلِّ أفقٍ — ودفَّ بوبلِ هاطلةٍ سكوبِ
يؤمُّ ثراكِ ـ مُزنةُ ـ إنَّ قلبي — تحمَّلَ كلَّ أحزانِ القلوبِ

SHELLS

Sails may dream of making peace with the wind
because in the beginning sails belonged to the kingdom of flowers and spirits.
Havens of peace ... where longings turn into songs;
colonies of colour .. spun from light and wind.
Miserable, endless roads may dream,
after a thousand or more sombre funeral processions,
of an eruption to light up new directions;
of oceans roaring, overflowing from man's innermost being.
For in the beginning, the sea was the absolute source of longings,
unlimited by the shores of time.
For in the beginning, the sea created waves and coral caves.
I dream of destroying walls and fences;
of bringing in a harvest of mystery;
of painting all that words and speech cannot express
and of silencing colours, shades and songs;
of etching the original which gives birth to other images;
of breaking open shells to free pearls as lovely as brides.

Abd al-Karim al-Tabbal
Morocco

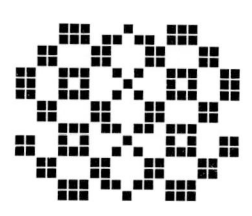

أصداف

شعر : عبد الكريم الطبّال
(المغرب)

إنْ يحلمِ الشّراعُ أنْ يسالمَ القلاعَ والرّياحْ
لأنّه في البدءِ كان من سلالةِ الأنهارِ والأرواحْ
معاقلِ السّلامِ... وملاحنِ الأشواقِ والأنغامْ
مزرعةِ الألوانِ.. مغزلِ الأضواءِ والأنسامْ
إنْ تحلمِ الشّوارعُ الحزينةُ المديدهْ
من بعدِ ألفٍ أو يزيدُ في جنازةٍ بليدهْ
أن يرسمَ البركانُ في لوحتِها مشاعلَ المسيرْ
أنْ يهدرَ البحرُ الكبيرُ، أنْ يفيضَ من دواخلِ الإنسانْ
لأنّه في البدءِ كان مطلقَ الأشواقِ
لاتّحدُ شواطئ الزّمانْ
لأنّه في البدءِ كان صانعَ الأمواجِ ومغاورِ المرجانْ
فإنّي أحلمُ أنْ أهدمَ الجدارَ والأسوارْ
أنْ أحصدَ الغلاتِ من مزارعِ الأسرارْ
أنْ أرسمَ الذي أعيا الحروفَ والكلامْ

وأخرسَ الألوانَ والظّلالَ والأنغامْ
أنْ أرسمَ الأصلَ الذي تليه سائرَ الصّورْ
أنْ أكسرَ الأصدافَ عن عرائسِ الدّررْ

THE REMAINS OF A PEARLING DHOW

(Excerpts)

You are merely remains
the grinding years have flung
to the earth as a testament
to future generations.
You regard the past, hidden behind a curtain of years,
as a lover who will return.
The millstones of the days have turned
pearling legends, sleeping in the depths of existence,
into stories to be sung.*

Cling to your memories since they bring consolation.
Remember the voice of the man who'd hum
and sing on your deck,*
while divers and their deckhands – those captives of the sea –
wore themselves out with work and worry, day after day.*

Remember the chanting
and the soft, evocative songs
filling the horizon with echoes of sadness
in faraway seas.
Remember those sails
opening the fullness of their arms to the wind,
like the wings of the whitest seagull,
as they struggled against the raging tempest.
Look at those ropes;
who knows how many hands they've slashed
like fearful swords.

بقايا سفينة غوص
شعر: مبارك بن سيف آل ثاني
(قطر)

مُقتطفات

إنّـمـا أنـتِ بقيّـة
قـد رمـاهـا الزمـنُ الطّـاحـنُ
للأرضِ وصيّـه
للصغـارِ القـادمـيـنْ
ترقُـبُ الأمسَ حبيبـاً عـائـداً
قـد توارى خلـف أستـارِ السنيـنْ
فلقـد دارتْ رحى الأيـامِ دورة
وغـدا الغـوصُ حكـايـاتٍ تُغنّـى
قصّـةً نـامـتْ بأعمـاقِ الوجـودْ

فاحفظي الذكرى ففي الذكرى عَـزاء
واستعيـدي صـوتَ «نهّـام»
علـى سطحِـكِ يشـدو بالغنـاء
وعليـه «السيـبُ» والغـوّاصُ أسرى
يمضيـانِ اليـومَ في همٍّ وكـدٍّ وعنـاء

واذكـري ذاكَ الـهـرجْ
والأغـاني الحـانيـه
تمـلأ الآفـاقَ أصـداءً وحُـزنـاً
في البحـارِ النـائيـه
واذكـري ذاكَ الشِّـراعْ
بـاسطـاً للـريـحِ ممـدودَ الـذِّراعْ
كجنـاحِ النـورسِ البـاهي البيـاضْ
هـو والإعصـارُ يمضي في صِـراعْ
وانظـري تلـكَ الحِـبـالْ
يـا ترى كـم مِـن يـدٍ قـد مزّقتها
كالسيـوفِ المـرعِـبـه

Remember the foaming water;
its cruel salt .. stinging bleeding wounds.
Remember the sun upon you,
the scorching wind
burning the humanity within you
and the pale faces.

Remembering all this, could you forget the last days of the diving season*
when dawn would bring new-born hope of reunion?
Remember the shore stretching out its arms,
and here the sand running towards you longingly after the pain of parting,
chiding and complaining that distance is unbearable.
Remember the past and tell yourself
this is the law of life.
How many lives are lived
and lost in the vast soils of time?
This is the law of life;
this is how life passes.

Mubarak Bin Saif Al Thani
Qatar

* Hikayaat: stories which are sung
* Naham: a man who would hum and sing to keep up the spirits of the divers.
* Ghawas: a diver who would collect pearl shells.
* Saib: man who would lower the divers.
* Gofal: closing days of the diving season.

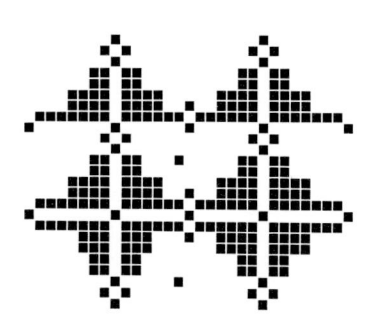

واذكري الماءَ الأُجاجْ
مِلحَه القاسي .. على تلكَ الجروحِ النادبهْ
واذكري الشمسَ عليكِ
والسَّمومَ اللاهبهْ
تحرقُ الإنسانَ فيكِ
والوجوهَ الشاحبهْ

إنْ تذكّرتِ فهل تنسينَ أيّامَ «القفّالْ»؟
وأتى الفجرُ وليداً في ثناياهُ الوصالْ
واذكري الشطَّ إذا ما الشطُّ قد مَدَّ ذراعهْ
وهفا الرملُ إليكِ في حنينٍ ووداعْ
عاتباً يشكو من البُعدِ التياعهْ
اذكري الأمسَ وقولي
إنها شَرعُ الحياةْ
كمْ حياةٍ عاشَها الدهرُ
وضاعتْ في ثراهْ
إنها شَرعُ الحياةْ
هكذا تمضي الحياةْ

EXISTENCE

I was to the world a wandering question.
                       In the closed unknown,
                       its answer was hiding.
You were for me a new ascending light,
                       raised from the darkness of the unknown
                       by destiny.
The stars circled with this light,
they circled twice,
until its unique radiance
reached me.   Darkness retreated
                       in two convulsions.
                       I found in my hand
                       my lost answer.
Oh you, oh you, so distant and so close,
                       don't speak of fading;
                       your spirit burns too fiercely.
The universe is mine and yours –
ours .. two poets,
in spite of immense distance,
have been joined by existence.

Fadwa Tuqan
Palestine

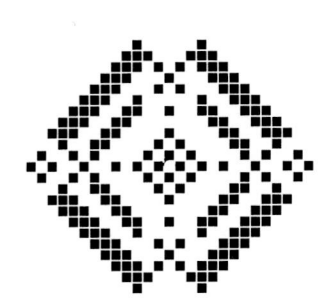

وجود
شعر: فدوى طوقان
(فلسطين)

كنتُ على الدنيا سؤالاً شريدْ
في الغيهبِ المسدولْ
جوابه استترْ
وكنتَ لي إشراقَ نورٍ جديدْ
من عتمةِ المجهولْ
أطلقه قدرْ

دارَ به الفلكْ
ودارَ مرتينْ
حتى انتهى إليَّ
إشعاعه الفريدْ
وانقشعَ الحلكْ
وفي انتفاضتينْ
وجدتُ في يديْ
جوابيَ الفقيدْ

يا أنتَ، يا أنتَ القريبَ البعيدْ
لا تذكرِ الأفولْ
روحُكَ تستعرْ

الكونُ لي ولكْ
لنا، لشاعرينْ
رغم المدى القصيّ
ضمّهما وجودْ

LOVE SONGS
(Excerpts)

How glorious it is .. when a man comes to life and grows
in the eyes of his beloved, forever.
So, after a shower over the eyes of the garden,
life begins anew in the fragrance
amidst the spring chatter of birds.
How wonderful is suffering,
how wonderful is suffering
for someone as cherished as the rain.
To wake up naked with the stars,
dreaming of a lovely woman whose eyelashes, brushed by the shadow of a cloud,
move to the rhythm of a song;
they dance, they dance above the smile of dusk.

The misery of man
doesn't exist among wild creatures in the wilderness;
doesn't exist in the landscape of wretchedness.
The misery of man begins when love for another
dies in his heart.

Azraj Umar
Algeria

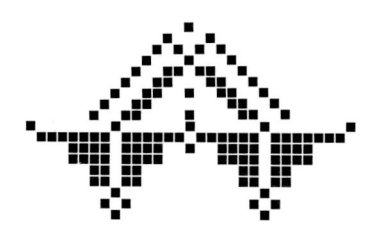

أغنيات حب
شعر: أزراج عمر
(الجزائر)

مُقتطفات

يا روعةً .. أن يزهر الإنسانْ
على رموشِ من يحبّه مدى الأزمانْ
فتسقطُ الأمطارُ فوق مقلةِ الحدائقْ
وتولدُ الحياةُ في العطورْ
ويلغطُ الربيعُ والطيورْ
ما أروعَ العذابْ
ما أروعَ العذابْ
من أجلِ إنسانٍ حببٍ كالمطرْ
يستيقظُ الإنسانُ عاريا مع النجومْ
ويَنسجُ الخيالُ عادةً رموشَها زفيرُ غيمْ
أهدابها تلويحةُ النغمْ
ويرقصان، يرقصانِ فوق بسمةِ الغسقْ

تعاسةُ الإنسانْ
ليست لدى وحشِ العراءْ
ليست على أرضِ الشقاءْ
تعاسةُ الإنسانِ أن يموتَ
في فؤادِه إنسانْ

THE ANSWER

Silence they said ... but I'm not dead;
        silence belongs to the lifeless.
The meaning of life is to speak and to act,
        in our sacred struggle ahead.*
While my heart beats and my tongue speaks,
        silence is not for me.
A nightingale sings wherever it is,
        in the highlands or the abyss;
this is the way I live my life,
        in spite of adversity.
In darkest cages, I believe,
        birds can sing joyfully.

Ibrahim al-Usta Umar
Libya

* Jihad: holy war.

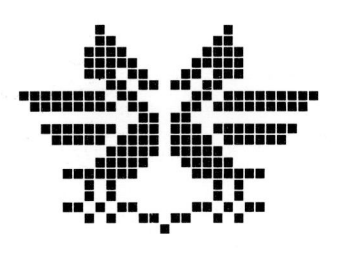

جواب

شعر: إبراهيم الأسطى عمر
ليبيا

قيلَ: صمتاً... فقلتُ لستُ بميتٍ
إنما الصمتُ ميزةٌ للجمادِ
إنّ معنى الحياةِ قولٌ وفعلٌ
وهي رمزٌ مقدّسٌ للجهادِ
لا أطيقُ السكوتَ مادامَ قلبي
خافقاً واللسانُ يروي مرادي
إنما البلبلُ المغرّدُ يشدو
أينما كانَ - في الربى في الوهادِ
ذاكَ دأبي مدى الحياةِ وإنّي
لا أبالي بما تجيءُ العوادي
لا أظنّ الأقفاصَ مهما ادلهمّتْ
تمنعُ الطيرَ لذةَ الإنشادِ

A DREAM OR A BET?
(Excerpts)

Let it be a dream
to hold the earth in my hands from ocean to ocean.
The earth is a violet or a red rose
which I fasten in the hair of my woman.
The hair of my woman is moons of gold and waves of flame.
The hair of my woman is wind, blue clouds, and the hair of my woman is rain.

Let it be a dream
to hold the earth in my lips from ocean to ocean.
The earth is bread or a cluster of grapes.
I pluck blue grapes for blue children
riding upon the hair of my woman.

Let it be a dream
to hold the earth in my heart from ocean to ocean.
The earth is blood
which I run over the hair of my woman.
The hair of my woman is rivers, blue water-wheels,
trees and blue poems
and orchards for the birth of blue wings.
The hair of my woman is blue horizons.

Muhammad Umran
Syria

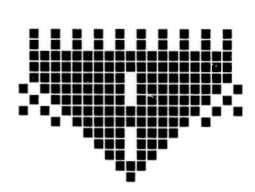

حلم؟ أمْ رهان؟

مقتطفات   شعر: محمّد عمران

(سوريا)

ليكنْ حلماً
إنّي أمسكُ في كفّي الأرضَ من الماءِ إلى الماءِ
الأرضُ بنفسجةٌ أو وردةُ جوري
إنّي أشكّلها في شعرِ امرأتي
شعرُ امرأتي أقمارٌ من ذهبٍ، أغمارٌ من لهبٍ
شعرُ امرأتي ريحٌ وغمائمُ زرقاءُ وشعرُ امرأتي مطرٌ

ليكنْ حلماً
إنّي أمسكُ في شفتيّ الأرضَ من الماءِ إلى الماءِ
الأرضُ رغيفٌ أو عنقودٌ
إنّي أفرطهُ عنباً أزرقَ للأطفالِ
الزرقِ الآتين على شعرِ امرأتي

ليكنْ حلماً
إنّي أمسكُ في قلبي الأرضَ من الماءِ إلى الماءِ
الأرضُ دمٌ
أجريهِ على شعرِ امرأتي
شعرُ امرأتي أنهارٌ وسواقٍ زرقٌ
أشجارٌ وقصائدُ زرقٌ
وبساتينُ لميلادِ الأجنحةِ الزرقِ
وشعرُ امرأتي آفاقٌ زرقٌ

THE CHILD IN ME

I've devoted my soul to art since I was a boy,
for artists view the world with bluest innocence and joy.
They consider God's a poet, who chooses dramatic themes,
providing parts to play for every human being
in the tragi-comedy of his poem called life.
Eve's primeval legend – snake, apple and bite –
echoes across aeons in poems and songs we write
and inscribe on fresh papyrus over the years,
to be soaked by those who suffer with ever-flowing tears.
These tears become pearls, giving inspiration
to those who change the world with each act of creation.

Ibrahim al-Urayyid
Bahrain

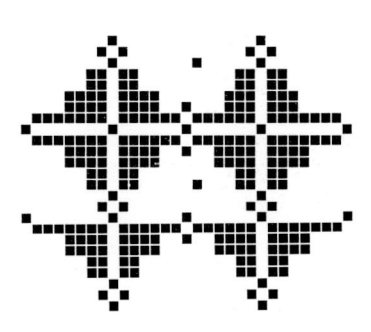

الطفل فيه
شعر: إبراهيم العريّض
(البحرين)

دنتُ بالفنّ صغيراً منذ شبّ الطفل فيه
لعبةً ترعى مجاليها العيون النرجسيّة
من رأى الخالقَ كالشاعر يختار رويّه
كلّما وقّع لحناً مثّلته البشريّة
فاذا المأساة والمهزلة أسمُ لقضيّه
هي اسطورةُ حواءِ جرت في إثر حيّه
إن ترجّعها طيور الخلد أنغاماً شجيّه
فهي في كوكبنا الأرضيّ أوراقٌ نديّه
طالما خضّلها دمعُ ضحايا المدنيّه
غير أن الدمع هذا قطراتٌ لؤلؤيّه
عطّر الفنّ ـ بما ندّت من زهرٍ ـ نديّه

THE NIGHT

Speak to me
oh twin soul,
speak to me,
for the fingers of night are fire
and my nerves are tempest-torn.
Unless you speak, I fear
a flame will consume you
and consume me.

Speak to me,
for the night is oriental fragrance,
a whisper of forgotten ages
and coloured images and shadows,
coursing through my blood,
lighting me up,
forging chains out of my thirst,
enticing me like a mirage,
to spread my hair like a waterfall
to hide you from the night and hide me.

Speak to me oh twin soul,
speak to me.
Close your eyes;
for them
I struggle between my doubt
and my certainty.
I fear looking into your eyes.
I surrender.

I escape from you, to you.
If I and the night rebel against you,
who would protect you,
who would protect me?

Thurayya al-Urayyid
Saudi Arabia

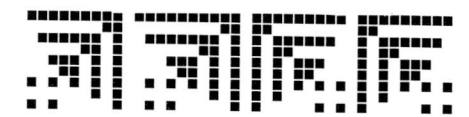

الليل
شعر: ثريا العريض
(المملكة العربية السعودية)

حدثني
يا توأم نفسي
حدثني
فالليلُ أصابعه نار
وأنا أعصابي أعصار
أخشى إن تصمتْ يستشري
لهبا يفنيك
ويفنيني

حدثني
فالليلُ عطورٌ شرقيةٌ
ونداءُ عصورٍ منسيةٍ
ألوانًا ترسم وظلالًا
تشري بدمي
تشعلني
تنحت من ظمأي أغلالًا
وتلوح سرابًا يغريني
إن أسدلَ شعري شلالًا
يخفيك عن الليلِ ويخفيني

حدثني يا توأم نفسي
حدثني
أغمض عينيك
فدا عينيك
صراعُ ظنوني
ويقيني
أخشى أن أنظرَ في عينيك
أنهار

فأهرب منكَ إليك
إن ثُرتُ أنا والليلُ عليك
مَن يحميك
مَن يحميني؟

A SACRED DAY

If I were God   I'd have changed the day
I met her into a miraculous day.
I'd have ordered the sun   to blaze triumphantly,
bathing the earth in light, dispelling darkness.
I'd have let all people give vent to their feelings
and be free on that day   to do as they wished,
so every soul   would feel fulfilled.
On that day I'd have asked forgiveness for all our sins.

Mahmud Abu al' Wafa
Egypt

يومٌ مقدّس
شعر: محمود أبو الوفا
(مصر)

آهِ يا يومَ لقاها   ليتني كنتُ إلهاً
كنتُ صيَّرتُك في الأيامِ يوماً لا يضاهي
لأمرتُ الشمسَ تبقى   فيكَ زهواً أضحاها
فاستحمّت في الضياءِ الأرضُ من جوْرِ دُجاها
ولَبَختُ الناسَ للناسِ خدوداً وشِفاها
فقضى الناسُ جميعاً   كلُّ نفسٍ مشتهاها
فإذا ما كلُّ نفسٍ   بلغتْ فيكَ مُناها
عُدتُ فاستغفرتُ للدنيا جميعاً من خطاها

THE DESERT

In the beginning the desert was
the ashes of a woman haunted by the fury of storms.
She uncovered what was hidden so the poet, reclining on the grass,
or sitting alone in the half-light,
could seek, in silence, something which had vanished
into her rusty mirrors.

In the beginning the language of the desert
was thrusting weeds flourishing against a wall of winds;
slender palms swaying in the season of fertility
and debris carried by the wind
to the blueness of warm sands.

Our first spring was our mother,
who carried us in her womb and delivered us
into the coming epoch of cities.

Al-Munsif al-Wahaybi
Tunisia

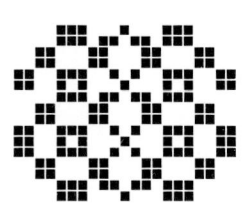

الصحراء
شعر: المنصف الوهايبي
تونس

كانتِ الصحراءُ مُ البدءِ
رمادَ إمرأةٍ مسكونةٍ بالعاصفة
تخرجُ الخِبءَ، فيستلقى على أعشابِها الشاعرُ
أو يجلسُ بين الظلِّ والنورِ وحيداً
صامتاً يبحثُ عن شيءٍ تلاشى
في مراياها الصديئة

لغةُ الصحراءِ مُ البدءِ
نخيلٌ طالعٌ يزهرُ في سورِ الرياح
ونخيلٌ فارعٌ يهتزُّ في فصلِ اللقاح
وغثاءٌ حملتْهُ الريحُ
حتى زرقةَ الرملِ الدفيئة

نبعُنا الأولُ كانتْ أمُّنا
حملتْنا ثمّ أهدتْنا
لعصرِ المدنِ المنتظرة

DROP OF SADNESS

All the fears of this world rest in my heart.
Who knows your frontiers, oh bird of fear?
Oh kingdom of fear,
abode of suffering.
        My love carries me;
I journey away from you
and I journey into you.
What a cross is my journey, extending to the far corners of the earth.
Oh my heart.
Oh bird exhausted by flight
still dragging bruised wings this way and that
across the earth.
Oh treasury of fear.
Oh drop of sadness,
beating above the cross of the world.
        Oh my heart!

Abd al-Razaq Abd al-Wahid
Iraq

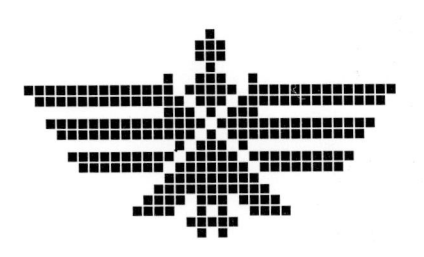

قطرةُ حُزْنٍ
شِعر: عبدالرزاق عبدالواحد
(العراق)

وطنٌ لمخاوفِ هذا العالمِ قلبي
من يعرفُ أين حدودكَ يا عصفورَ الخوفْ؟
يا مملكةَ الخوفِ
وطنٌ للآلامِ
ويحملني حبي
أرحلُ منكَ
وأرحلُ فيكَ
أيُّ صليبٍ يمتدُّ إلى أطرافِ الأرضِ رحيلي
يا قلبي
يا طيراً أنهكهُ الطوفْ
ولم يبرحْ يسحبُ في كلِّ جهاتِ الأرضِ
جناحيهِ المسحوقين
يا كنزَ الخوفْ
يا قطرةَ حُزْنٍ
تنبضُ فوقَ صليبِ العالمَ
يا قلبي!

SAILING WITH THE WIND

Oh sailors .. from your eyes,
I seem to see you drowning,
You're like trees whose leaves
or whose trunks become bowed
The tattered clothes that cling
how often I've stitched them up,
The wind is carrying you west,
whenever your eyes are burning,
You always have my heart,

rivers of love are flowing.
you've been lost and at sea so long.
are shrivelled by hard winter
and scorched in their nakedness.
to your skin are never removed;
while covering you with mine.
while I sail east with you;
I'll scatter you with flowers.
the oil in your lamp at night.

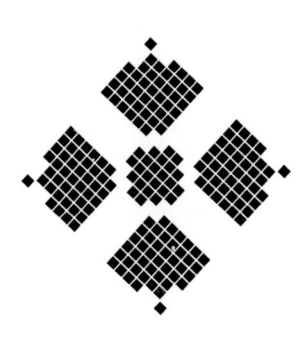

Khalifa al-Wuqayyan
Kuwait

المبحرون مع الرياح
شعر: خليفة الوقيان
(الكويت)

يا مبحرون.. وفي محاجركم   نهرانِ من نبع الهوى شُقّا
إني لألمحكم وإن عبثت   طال السرى بمتاهةٍ غرقى
أوراقكم في غصنها يبست   ويدُ الشتاء تذيبها سحقا
وجذوعكم عريانة سجدت   والريح تحرق عريها حرقا
أثوابكم مزق وما خلعت   حتى مَ فوق جلودكم تبقى؟
كم رحت أخلع فوقها جزعا   ثوبي، وكم لململتها رتقا
الريح تسرح في شراعكم   غربا، وأبحركم شرقا
إني سأرشقكم إذا حُرقت   أجفانكم بأزاهري رشقا
قلبي لكم في كل مفترقٍ   زيت السراج بليلكم يُسقى

TONIGHT WE WAKE YOU WITH ROSES

Tonight .. we light a lamp .. we come to you,
one by one, circling your pillow .. watching;
flocks of ducks flying over your closed eyes
on their quick flight into exile.
What kind of drowsiness is breaking
over your eyes,
clear as spring water,
calm as spring water,
free-flowing as spring water?
What kind of drowsiness can this be
when flocks of ducks arrive
and fly away
and your sails do not depart?
We gather around you.
More rivers than one still trace a way
between those lips, so speak to us.
Who told you the country moon would die,
the heart would die
and the child of love would die?
Who told you seas abuse seagulls,
that the shore doesn't embrace each breaking wave, nor give
shells to children?
No one told you.
The earth is your cloak of warmth in the rain,
the grass your sleeping place,
the hair of the women you've loved a pillow for your sleep.
You are time .. water,
the kingdom,
so how could you die?

Isa al-Yasiri
Iraq

نُوقظُكِ الليلةَ بالورد
شعر : عيسى الياسري
(العراق)

الليلةَ .. نُوقِدُ قنديلاً .. ونحنّي إليكِ
تباعاً نخلقُ حول وسادة نومكِ .. نرقبُ
أسراب البط عتراً قريباً من عينيكِ
المغمضتين وترحلُ مسرعةً صوبَ المنفى
أيُّ نعاسٍ هذا المتكسرُ
فوقَ العينين
الصافيتين كنبعٍ
الهادئتين كنبعٍ
والراكضتين كنبعٍ
أيُّ نعاسٍ هذا
أن تأتي أسرابُ البط
وترحلَ ثانيةً
وشراعُكِ لا يُقلعُ

إنا نتجمعُ حولكِ
أكثرَ من نهرٍ مازال يشقُ طريقاً
عبر مسالك هاتين الشفتين .. فخذتنا
من قال بأن القمرَ الربيعَ يموتْ؟
والقلبَ يموتْ؟
وصبيَّ الحب يموتْ؟
من قال بأن الحرَ يشاكسُ طائرْ
والشاطئ لا يحتضنُ الموجةَ أو يُعطي
صدفاً للأطفالْ؟
لا أحدٌ قالْ
الأرضُ عباءةُ دفئكِ إذ تنتشي الدنيا
العشبُ فراشكِ
شعرُ المعشوقات وسادةُ نومكِ
أنتِ الزمنُ .. الماءُ
الملكوتُ
فكيف تموتْ؟

GRIEF

Last night he passed her in the desert –
that river of undulating sand, silent wind and echoes.
He was watching a star; its light
concealed like water,
distant like water,
cold like water.
He passed her last night as darkness bowed its head.
His abandoned house was grieving in the desert;
even the silence of the garden was consumed by the wind.
Oh drop of water!
Call at his house, call
and ask about her. Oh ... oh, if only she knew
how black are the nights without her;
that I am here like a drop of water,
in the night ... in a desert.

Sa'di Yusuf
Iraq

كآبة

شعر: سعدي يوسف
(العراق)

مرَّ بها أمسِ، وكان الليلُ في الصحراءْ
نهراً من الموج الترابيّ، وصمتُ الريحِ والأصداءْ
كان يرى نجماً، ولكنْ كانتِ الأضواءْ
دفينةً كالماءْ
بعيدةً كالماءْ
باردةً كالماءْ
مرَّ بها أمسِ، وفي إطراقة الظلماءْ
منزلهُ المهجورُ يبكي، يسكنُ الصحراءْ
حديقةٌ تنهشُ حتى صمتها الأنواءْ
يا قطرةً من ماءْ!
مرِّي على منزله مرِّي
ولتسألي عنها، وآهِ... آهِ لو تدري
أنَّ الليالي بعدها سوداءْ
إني هنا قطرةُ من ماءْ
في الليل... في صحراءْ

MOMENTS OF INSPIRATION

(Excerpts)

I feel the winds of Paradise
soon rhymes are stirring,
This one slips away,
another departs in despair;
I scatter them across the world,
for when they touch my soul
I pour into my poems
to people the world with nations.
dazed yet caring and joyful,
Had I not known these symptoms
blowing through the depths of my soul;
ant-like in my mind.
that one submits responding,
now this one's promising.
in their fragrant innocence;
and I am deeply moved,
the essence of all dreams,
I surrender to my rhymes,
as I listen in peace or anger.
of genius, I'd rush to a doctor.

Muhammad Mahmud al-Zubairi
North Yemen

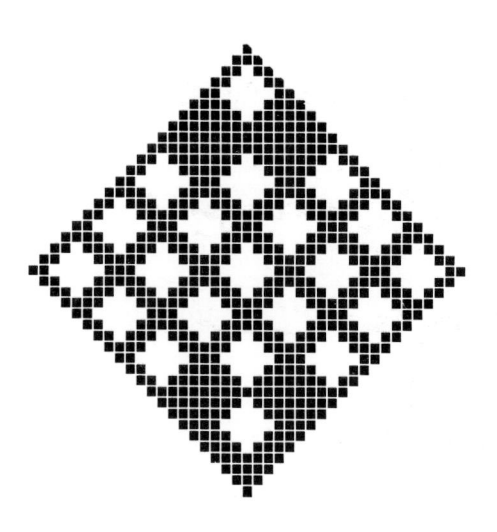

لحظات الإشراق

شعر: محمّد محمود الزبيري
(اليمن)

مقتطفات

أُحسُّ بريحٍ كريحِ الجنانِ .... تهبُّ بأعماقِ روحي هبوبا
وأشعرُ أنَّ القوافي تدبُّ .... كالنملِ ملءَ دماغي دبيبا
فهذا ينزُّ وهذا يروغُ .... وذلكَ يذعنُ لي مستجيبا
وذاكَ يفارقُني يائساً .... وهـذا يواعدُني أن يؤوبا
ومنهـا أوزعُ للعـالمينَ .... طهراً وأنشرُ في الأرضِ طيبا
إذا لمستْ مهجتي لمسةٌ .... توثّبَ قلبي بصَدْري وثوبا
أُخلّفُ فيها لقاحَ المنى .... وأُنجبُ للأرضِ منها شعوبا
أُسلّمُ نفسي لهـا ذاهلاً .... حريصاً عليها بشوشاً طروبا
وأُصغي لها هـادِئاً تارةً .... وأحرصُ حيناً عبوساً غضوبا
ولولا اهتدائي لسرِّ النبوغِ .... وإعراضِه لطلبتُ الطبيبا

NOTES ON THE POETS

LUTFI JA'FAR AMAN (1928-1972) Born in Aden, S.Yemen, educated Khartoum, Sudan. Worked as a teacher in Aden, then as Deputy Minister of Education and Supervisor of Broadcasting. Influenced by Tunisian and Sudanese Romantic poets, he became a leader of modern Romantic poetry in Yemen. 5 volumes published. Died in Cairo.

LAME'A ABBAS AMARA Born in the 1930s in Amara, Iraq, where she finished school. Graduated from Teachers Training College in Baghdad in 1950. Writes classical and modern poetry and has published 3 volumes. Lives in California and London.

HILAL AL-AMIRI (1957 -) Born at Samayel in central Oman. On administrative staff of Sultan Qaboos University, Muscat. A modernist.

SA'ID AQL (1912 -) Born in Zahla, this nationalist Lebanese poet is often called the first symbolist Arab poet. In fact he is more of a Romantic, though emphasising joy in his verse. His work, first as romanticist then as symbolist, greatly influenced the new generation of poets.

HASAN FATH AL-BAB Born in Egypt in the 1920s; began his career in the police force, worked his way through university to obtain a PhD in law. Now teaches in Algeria. Has published 7 volumes of social realist poetry.

SHAWQI BAGHDADI (1928 -) Born in Banyas on the Syrian coast. Graduated in Arabic studies from Damascus University and has since taught Arabic literature in Syrian secondary schools. Since the 1950s has contributed to many Syrian and other Arab periodicals, writing poetry, short stories, literary articles. Has published 4 anthologies of poetry and 2 of short stories. One of the founders of the "Syrian Writers Association" in the 1950s, thus supporting progressive literary objectives in modern Syria. Active in radical politics and an outspoken defender of freedom.

HAMRI BAHRI (1947 -) Born in Algiers. Taught Arabic at high schools then moved into literary journalism. On editorial boards of literary journals "Al-Ru'ya" and "Amal" and board of Algerian Writers Union. Poems from his 2 volumes have been translated into French and Russian. He is a modernist.

ABDULLAH AL-BARADUNI (1929 -) Born in Baraddun in north Yemen and restricted by blindness contracted after smallpox at age 6. Nevertheless excelled in studies, graduating in Arabic Language and Sharia in 1952. Has taught, but now works in cultural section of Broadcasting Service in Sanaa. Has published at least 8 collections of poetry.

ABD AL-WAHAB AL-BAYATI (1926 -) Born in Baghdad and educated Baghdad Teachers Training College. Once member of Iraqi Communist Party but resigned for ideological reasons. Worked as schoolteacher, journalist and diplomat. Enjoys great popularity. Writes in free verse and is generally regarded as leader of social realist movement in modern Arabic poetry. Has been published in several volumes of Collected Poems.

BABHA BIN BEDAYWAH (1966 -) Born in the Mauritanian desert near a well which is now the site of a village. Tended goats and sheep as a shepherd, then went to live in the city where he now attends university and writes poetry, some of which has been published.

MAHMUD DARWISH (1942 -) Born in al-Barwa, a village east of Acre; lived in Haifa where he edited a bi-weekly newspaper and wrote poems against Zionist rule. Has suffered imprisonment and house arrest. In 1969 he won the Lotus Prize and received it from Indira Ghandi during the 1970 Afro-Asian Writers Conference in New Delhi. Lived in Beirut from 1971 to 1982 and now lives in Paris where he edits the literary journal al-Karmal. A very well known poet, he has published many volumes of poetry and was awarded the Lenin Prize in 1983.

AMAL DUNQAL (1940 - 1983) Born in a village of upper Egypt and went to Cairo in the 1960s. Began publishing poetry and under the influence of the city changed from a semi-Romantic to a social realist. Published 5 collections of poetry. Lived lavishly and was known by fellow poets as "the tramp" from his love of the "free life". Died after 4 years of illness in the National Tumour Institute where he composed an extraordinary volume entitled "Papers of Room 8".

MUHAMMAD HASAN FAQI (1912 -) Born in Mecca, studied there and in Jeddah. Became teacher then newspaper editor. Later served government of Saudi Arabia in various capacities including ambassador to Indonesia. Retired to write several volumes of poetry as well as short stories and books on literary, religious and legal matters.

MUHAMMAD AL-FAYIZ (1938 -) Born in Kuwait, works in literary section of Radio and Television in Ministry of Information. Published first collection of poetry in 1964 and has since published several other collections, much of it marked by nostalgia for the days before oil brought wealth.

ABDULLAH AL-FAYSAL (1922 -) Born in Riyadh, son of King Faysal of Saudi Arabia. Studied in Hijaz and became Minister of Health and Minister of the Interior. Eventually left government to concentrate on business - and writing poetry, being known as the poet-prince. Has published two collections of verse, mostly love poems.

MUHAMMAD AL-FAYTURI (1930 -) Born and educated in Alexandria, Egypt. Father Sudanese, mother Egyptian. Moved to Cairo and published several volumes of poetry, much concerned with the feelings of a black man in a world dominated by whites.

MUHAMMAD ABDUH GHANIM (1922 -) Born in Aden and studied there and in London. Became a teacher, then diplomat and later supervisor of education. Has published 3 volumes of classical poetry and a play.

MUHAMMAD AL-GHAZZI (1949 -) Born in Tunis where he teaches in high school. Began poetical career by publishing militant poetry in modernist style. Has been gaoled several times. First anthology published 1957.

QASIM HADDAD (1948 -) Born in Bahrain and though self-educated has become one of leading poets of the Gulf region. Has published several collections of modernist poetry and is now Director of Culture and Art at Ministry of Information.

BULAND AL-HAIDARI (1926 -) Born in Iraq of Kurdish family, political activist under Iraqi monarchy. Lives in exile in Beirut where he works as journalist and bookshop manager. Has published several collections of poetry.

"SARAH HARIB" (1959? -) Pen name of a poet usually resident in Dubai. She graduated from the Emirates University and now studies journalism for a post-graduate degree form Cairo University. Has had poems published in journals and newspapers.

MUHAMMAD AL-HARITHI (1961 -) Born at al-Mudhairib in Shakiya, Oman. Graduated in geology from Doha University in Qatar. Has been writing surrealistic free verse since 1982.

ZAFIR AL-HASAN (1936 -) Born in al-Koora, Lebanon. Obtained PhD in law from the Sorbonne. WIdely travelled as a diplomat, he has written modernist verse and translated from French.

KHALIL HAWI (1925 -) Born in Shuwair, Lebanon; educated at American University in Beirut, then at Cambridge, England. Became Professor of Arabic Literature at American University of Beirut and is highly regarded as powerful, often symbolist poet.

AHMAD ABD AL-MU'TI HIJAZI (1935 -) Born in a village of the Nile Delta, he studied at the Teachers College in Cairo. He developed militant socialist tendencies, reflected in his social realist poetry which is often concerned with the bewilderment of poor villagers in the big city. He has published 2 volumes of poetry.

MUHAMMAD AL-MAKKI IBRAHIM (1944 -) Born in Western Sudan, he graduated from the University of Khartoum and continued with post-graduate studies in Paris. For 20 years a diplomat, he is now director for western Europe in the Ministry of Foreign Affairs. He writes free verse and has published one volume of poetry.

SAMA' ISA (1954 -) He is headmaster of a high school in Muscat, Oman. A surrealist poet, he has published one volume of poetry in the USA and another in Paris.

BADAWI AL-JABBAL (1900 - 1981) His real name, Muhammad Sulaiman al-Ahmad, was overshadowed by his literary name. Born in Difa, Lattaqia in Northern Syria, his father was a well educated religious leader of the Alawite sect. The poet was elected to parliament several times after independence and became Minister for Health and Minister for Information. He is an outstanding neo-classical poet whose 3 volumes of poetry have run into many editions.

MUHAMMAD MAHDI AL-JAWAHIRI (1900 -) Born in Najaf in Iraq and brought up by a well educated family, he studied traditional Islamic sciences and learned much about Arabic poetry. Moving to Baghdad, he worked as a teacher and journalist and edited revolutionary papers. Because of his political views he has several times been forced to live in exile. Always a fervent opponent of despotism, he has found it difficult to settle for long in some Arab countries and for more than 20 years has moved between Czechoslovakia, Iraq and Syria. An outstanding neo-classical poet, his prolific work often reflects his political adventures and his 8 volumes of poetry have been reprinted many times.

SALMA AL-KHADRA AL-JAYYUSI (1922 -) Born in Safad in northern Palestine, she was educated at Schmidt's Girls College in Jerusalem and at the American University of Beirut. She gained a PhD from London University and has travelled widely with her Jordanian diplomat husband. A teacher and literary journalist, she now lives in the USA where, as well as writing fine lyrical poetry, she is active in translating Arabic literature into English. She has had several volumes of poetry published and, among many other works, translated into Arabic Archibald MacLeish's "Poetry and Experience".

ILYAS KHALIL JURYIS (1946 -) Born Taibeh, near Irbid, Joran. Graduated in Arabic literature Beirut Arab University. Worked as a schoolteacher and journalist before retiring for health reasons.

YUSUF AL-KHAL (1917 - 1987) Born in Tripoli, Lebanon, he graduated at American University of Beirut where he then taught for a few years. In 1947 became editor of "Sawt al-Mar'ah" journal. From 1948 to 1955 worked as journalist at UN in New York. Returned to teach at American University of Beirut and in 1957 founded "Majallat Shi'r" (Poetry Review), which became leading forum for free verse poetry. Now an editor with Dar al-Nahar publishing house in Beirut. Has translated Eliot, Pound, Frost and others and has published several volumes of poetry.

BISHARAH AL-KHURI (1885 - 1968) Born in Beirut, gained a solid grounding in classical Arab literature and studied 19th century French romantic poetry, from which he made several translations. Known also as Al-Akhtal al-Saghir, a pen name denoting his Arab nationalism. Worked as a journalist, founded the periodical "al-Barq", and became President of the syndicate of journalists. Famous throughout the Arab world for his poetry which is romantic and relies heavily on the old Arab heritage for its themes.

SALAH LABAKI (1906 - 1955) Born in Brazil but brought as a baby to Lebanon where he studied at Hikmah College in Beirut and at `Aynturah. Founded the Lebanese literary society Ahl al-Qalam and became a leading symbolist poet. Published 5 volumes of verse.

HASAN AL-LAWZI (1952 -) Born in Sanaa, North Yemen, studied at al-Azhar University in Cairo and held important government posts, including Minister of Culture, in Sanaa. Has published several volumes of poetry and short stories, many deeply concerned with the Yemeni revolution.

ILIYA ABU MADI (1889 - 1957) Born in Lebanon and moved as a child to Egypt. Received little formal education and worked as a tobacconist until 1911 when he published his first volume of poetry. In 1916 emigrated to the USA where, while working in business, he wrote poems and articles and joined Gibran Khalil Gibran's literary circle. A Mahjar poet, he published two more volumes of verse and established "al-Samir", a literary fortnightly which became a daily in 1936. He edited this until his death and meanwhile published a further two volumes of poetry.

HAYDAR MAHMUD (1938 -) Born in Haifa, is a graduate of the University of California Los Angeles and an honorary PhD from the International Academy of Culture and Arts. One of his 7 poetry collections was awarded the Spanish Poetry Award in 1986. Started publishing in 1969 while journalist with Jordan TV. Appointed Director General of Culture and Arts and lately Cultural Adviser to the Prime Minister of Jordan.

ALI MIRZA MAHMUD (1952 -) Born in Doha, Qatar and graduate of Doha University. Works in TV section of Ministry of Information and has been actor and theatre director since 1972; co-founder of the Qatari Theatre Group. A modernist poet, he has published 3 collections of poems.

AHMAD AL-MAJATI (1930s? -) Born in Casablanca, Morocco and educated at Muhammad V University, Rabat, where he is now a professor in the Faculty of Letters. A modernist poet.

JA'FAR MAJID (1940 -) Born at Kairouan, Tunisia, graduated from University of Tunis in Arabic Literature in 1963 then studied further at University of Paris. Now a professor in University of Tunis and has published 2 volumes of poetry, having moved from neo-classical romanticism to modernism.

NAZIK AL-MALA'IKAH (1923 -) Born in Baghdad to a poet mother, popularly known as Um Nizar, who was an early nationalist in the fight against British colonialism in Iraq. Nazik al-Mala'ikah studied at the Teachers College in Baghdad, then studied English Literature at Princeton, USA, before returning to teach successively at Musil and Basra Universities. She is now professor of Arabic Literature at the University of Kuwait. She has published numerous collections and is a leader of the free verse movement.

SHAFIQ AL-MA'LUF (1905 -) Born in Zahla, Lebanon, and in 1922 moved with family to Damascus where his father was a member of the Arab Language Academy. Published first collection of romantic poetry in 1926 before joining his brother Fawzi in Brazil where he became a wealthy businessman. Led the major grouping of South American Mahjar poets and is famous for early attempts to establish the art of the epic in Arabic poetry.

ABD AL-AZIZ AL-MAQALIH (1939 -) Born in North Yemen, studied at University of Cairo and returned to become active promoter of Yemeni literature and culture. President of Sanaa University and of the Centre for Yemeni Studies. Famous as a modernist poet throughout Arab world, he has published many collections of poetry and in 1986 was awarded the Lotus Prize for literature.

AHMAD MATAR (1950 -) Born in Basra, spent his youth in Kuwait where he worked as journalist and published modernist poetry. Has had 3 volumes of verse published and now works for the Arabic press in London, writing a regular column on Arabic poetry.

AHMAD AL-SAFI AL-NAJAFI (1894 -?) Born in Najaf, Iraq, he spent several years as a young man in Iran where he studied Persian and translated Omar Khayyam into Arabic. Left Iraq for Lebanon and published several volumes of neo-classicist poetry.

IBRAHIM NAJI (1898 - 1953) Born in Cairo, he became a medical practitioner and a fluent linguist, speaking English, French and German, and studying romantic poetry of French and English poets. Wrote 3 volumes of romantic verse which greatly influenced Arabic poetry in the 1930s and 1940s.

IBRAHIM NASRALLAH (1954 -) Born to a Palestinian family in Israel, attended the UNWRA Teachers Institute then went to teach for 2 years in Saudi Arabia. Since 1978 has worked as a literary journalist and has published 6 collections of poems, a novel (translated into English) and a prose-poem on the Palestinian uprising.

ISA AL-NA'URI (1918 - 1985) Born in Na'ur, Jordan. Studied at Clerical School in Jerusalem and taught in schools from 1954 - 1975. Edited the literary journal "Al-Salaam al-Jadeed" (The New Pen) and published 26 books including novels, collections of Arabic literature and 3 collections of poetry. Went to Italy to study Italian literature in 1960. In 1976 was awarded honorary doctorate by University of Palermo for translations of Italian literature into Arabic. Was a member of the Arabic Language Academy in Amman, Jordan.

NIZAR QABBANI (1923 -) Born in Damascus, Syria, where he graduated from law school of Damascus University. Worked in diplomatic service until resigning to establish a publishing house in Beirut. A prolific and popular poet, he is the author of 25 collections of poetry as well as an autobiography.

SAMIH AL-QASIM (1939 -) Born in Zarqa, Jordan, of a Palestinian family from Rama in Galilee. Grew up and was educated in Rama and Nazareth. A political activist against Israeli rule, he has been gaoled several times. Now lives in Haifa, runs the Arabesque Press and the Palestinian Folk Art Centre. Author of 25 volumes of modernist poetry, an autobiographical novel and a published diary.

HASAN ABDULLAH AL-QURASHI (1926 -) Born in Mecca and graduated from University of Riyadh (now King Saud University). Served in several high government positions and as ambassador. A famous book-collector, he has published widely in Saudi and pan-Arab journals. Has published 3 collections of poetry, one of them in 2 volumes.

GHAZI AL-QUSAIBI [Al-Gosaibi] (1940 -) Born in eastern Saudi Arabia, went as a young boy, after his mother's early death, to Bahrain where he went to school. Graduated in law from the University of Cairo, then in International Relations (MA) from University of Southern California and was awarded PhD in Political Science from London University in 1978. Has served Saudi government as Minister of Industry and Electricity and Minister of Health and is currently Saudi Arabian ambassador to Bahrain. Has published 8 volumes of poetry and several anthologies of Arabic verse.

ABD AL-RAHMAN RAFI' (1938 -) Born and educated in Bahrain, he writes folk poetry as well as formal poetry in both the traditional form and as free verse. Has published several volumes of poetry.

GEELI ABD AL-RAHMAN (1931 -) Born in great poverty in the Sudan, he joined his father at the age of 9 in Cairo. Much influenced by his childhood in the slums of Cairo, he became a social realist poet and now lectures at the University of Algeria, having received a PhD from Moscow University. A noted literary critic with several volumes of poetry to his credit.

ABD AL-MUN'IM AL-RIFA'I (1916 - 1986) Born in Tyre, Lebanon, and graduated from American University of Beirut in 1937. Schoolteacher in Amman, Jordan, and became secretary to Prince Abdullah before Kingdom of Jordan was established; later became Information Minister and subsequently held other ministries and ambassadorial posts as well as serving as Prime Minister of Jordan. Published one collection of poems.

UMAR ABU RISHAH (1910 -) Born in Aleppo and studied at American University of Beirut, then in England where he studied and was influenced by English romantic poetry. Became librarian in Aleppo, then held a number of diplomatic posts. Considered to be one of the great Arab romantic poets, but much of his work remains unpublished.

ADIB SA'B (1945 -) Born in Beirut, his father published for over 40 years a review for colloquial Lebanese poetry and folklore and is regarded as Lebanon's poet laureate in colloquial verse. Adib Sa'b graduated from American University of Beirut and from London University. Became lecturer in philosophy at American University of Beirut and professor of philosophy at St John of Damascus School of Theology in Balaman University (North Lebanon). Lived in London and Paris, consultant for UN organisations, and editor-in-chief of "Al-Azmina", cultural pan-Arab bi-monthly. Has published 2 collections of poems.

ALI AL-SAB'TI (1934 -) Born in Kuwait and studied at its oldest school. Former editor-in-chief of "Al-Yaqza" magazine, he is a journalist and writer and former boardmember of the Writers Association. Writes regularly on poetry for Kuwaiti literary journals and has published 2 collections of poetry.

SALAH ABD AL-SABUR (1934 -) Born in Egypt, studied at Cairo University, and was introduced to Western literature by Lewis 'Awad. Has been deeply influenced by T.S.Eliot. Moved from romantic beginnings to social realism and is author of several volumes of poetry, essays and verse plays. He is editor of a monthly journal and director of a state publishing house.

ALI AHMAD SA'ID (1930 -) Born in Qassabin, Syria, and graduated from Syrian University in Damascus. Has lived in Beirut since 1956, apart from a year at the Sorbonne in Paris, and publishes his own magazine interested in all issues of Arab life. Early in his career as a poet, he adopted the pen name "Adonis" and has published several volumes of verse and prose-poems as well as a 3-volume anthology of classical Arabic poetry.

MUHAMMAD AL-AKHDAN AL-SA'IHI (1917 -) Born in the Algerian desert, he graduated in Islamic and Arabic studies from the University of Zitouna, worked in Algerian broadcasting and then took a post as counsel to the Minister of Religious Affairs. His classical poetry has been translated into Russian and French. He has published 4 volumes of verse and is now retired.

AHMAD SALIH AL-SALIH (1946 -) Born in Unaiza in Qassim, Saudi Arabia, went to school in Runya then moved to Taif in 1960. Graduated from Imam Muhammad ibn Saud University in Riyadh in which city he now works as a public servant. His pen name is al-Musafir (The Traveller). He has published 3 volumes of modernist poetry.

"RUA SALIM" Pen name of a poet born in the United Arab Emirates in about 1957. She is now studying psychology in the USA; her poetry is modern and filled with nostalgia.

NURRADIN SAMMUD (1932 -) Born at Kelibia in Tunisia, he completed secondary studies at the University of Zitouna and took a higher degree at Cairo University in the Faculty of Letters. Studied further at the Lebanese University in Beirut where he won the Poetry Prize in 1959. Now a professor at the University of Tunis, he is also a literary critic and prolific poet. He began as a romantic poet, then joined the modernists.

MUHAMMAD AL-SARGHINI (1930 -) Born at Fez in Morocco;

educated at Al-Qarawiyyeen University and Baghdad University, then gained his doctorate from the Sorbonne. Became an academic and started his poetic career under the influence of the Mahjar poets of the Americas. Has published 5 collections of free verse and is now Vice Dean of the Faculty of Arts and Science at Fez University.

GEORGE SAYDAH (1893 - 1978) Born the son of a judge in the old quarter of Damascus, he was later educated in Lebanon and then lived in Cairo until 1925. Moved to Paris and eventually emigrated to Venezuela, and from there moved to Argentina. Finally settled in Beirut in 1954. Researched the work of the Mahjar poets and was himself both poet and essayist.

HABIB AL-SAYEGH (1955 -) Born in Abu Dhabi, graduated from the University of Alexandria and worked in the Ministry of Information, then in journalism. Author of several volumes of poetry, he edits "Awraq" literary review which was founded in London in 1983.

YUSUF AL-SAYEGH (1932 -) Born in Mowsil, Iraq, and a graduate of the Higher Teachers Training College in Baghdad. Has published several volumes of verse which take further the modern developments of Arabic poetry in the 1950s. He is Director General of Cinema and Theatre in Iraq and is a novelist, artist, dramatist and poet.

BADR SHAKIR AL-SAYYAB (1926 - 1964) The little village of Jaykur in Iraq was the subject of much of his poetry in which he set out to free Arabic verse from many of its traditional shackles. Educated in Basra and at the Teachers Training College in Baghdad. Worked as a school teacher and was dismissed and exiled for his political views. Started as a romantic poet, became a social realist, and is regarded by many as the greatest poet of his generation for his symbolist poetry, strongly influenced by T.S.Eliot and Edith Sitwell. Died in Kuwait after a serious illness.

ILYAS ABU SHABAKAH (1903 - 1947) Born in New York and educated in Lebanon. Widely read in French literature, he became a romantic poet and a journalist. Published several volumes of verse and many translations from French classical and romantic literature. Generally regarded as Lebanon's leading romantic poet.

AHMAD AL-SHARIF (1872 - 1959) Born in Tripoli, Libya, he emigrated after the Italians invaded Libya before World War I. Returned in 1922 to his position as a judge and rose to highest judicial office (Lord Justice) in 1943. During Libya's struggle for independence, his poetry became very nationalistic, but remained classical in form. Known as the Prince of Poets.

ALI AL-SHARQAWI (1948 -) Born in Manama, Bahrain and studied at the University of Baghdad. Studied veterinary science in Britain and now works at the veterinary laboratory in Manama. An experimental poet working from the modernist tradition, he has published at least 7 volumes of poetry and is Chairman of the Bahraini Union of Writers.

MUHAMMAD IBRAHIM ABU SINNAH (1937 -) Born in Egypt and studied at Al-Azhar University. Much travelled, he now works in Radio Cairo's cultural section. In his 6 anthologies and 3 verse dramas, he shows a change from romanticism to social realism. He writes critical essays on contemporary poetry.

HUSAIN SIRHAN (1913 -) Born in Mecca, he left school early and is largely self-taught. Has worked in various government posts and became famous for his revolutionary ideas as well as for his classical style poetry.

ABD AL-KARIM AL-TABBAL (1931 -) Born at Chauven in Morocco and graduated from Fez University to become a teacher. A classical poet at first, he is now a modernist. Has published an anthology of poetry and a poetic drama.

MUBARAK BIN SAIF AL THANI (1950 -) Born in Doha, Qatar and graduated in Arabic literature from Cairo University and in economics in the USA. Works in the Qatari Ministry of Foreign Affairs. Was awarded the 1985 prize for poetry by the Spanish-Arab Institute for Culture and Art.

FADWA TUQAN (1917 -) Born and educated in Nablus, Palestine, she was introduced to verse-writing by her brother Ibrahim, a well known poet. Her early poems were romantic and written in traditional form, but later she wrote in free verse. The issue of resistance dominated her work after her home town fell under Israeli occupation in June 1967. She has published several volumes of poetry.

AZRAJ UMAR (1949 -) Born in the Algerian village of Tizi Rashed, studied Arabic at high school and became a teacher and later a journalist in London. Belongs to the "angry generation". Has published 3 collections of poems, many of which have been translated into Russian, French, Serbo-Croatian, Vietnamese, Spanish and German.

IBRAHIM AL-USTA UMAR (1907 - 1950) Born in Darna, Libya, and self-educated, he was always poor. Fled to Egypt during Italian occupation before World War II, then lived in Syria, Iraq, Palestine and Jordan. Enlisted in the Sanusian Liberation Army and was drowned at sea. His poetry was classical but with a modern feeling. It has been collected in a single volume.

MUHAMMAD UMRAN (1943 -) Born in Drikeesh, Northern Syria, studied Arabic at Damascus University and worked in literary journalism. Is now editor of "Al-Ma'rifa" monthly. Has published many anthologies and is regarded as one of the outstanding representatives of modern poetry.

IBRAHIM AL-URAYYID (1908 -) Born in India, the son of a Bahraini father and an Iraqi mother, he lost his mother while still an infant and was brought up with the help of Indian women in Bombay where his father was a pearl merchant. Returning to Bahrain at age 20, he studied Arabic and, though his first attempts at verse were in Urdu and English, he quickly excelled in his parental tongue and published several books of literary criticism as well as poetry.

THURAYA AL-URAYYID (1946 -) Born in Bahrain and the 6th daughter of Ibrahim al-Urayyid. Graduated from the American University of Beirut, then a PhD from the University of North Carolina, Chapel Hill, USA. Now lives in Saudi Arabia with her husband and gives radio and TV lectures on education, women, social and literary events. Her first collection of modern poetry is due to be published shortly.

MAHMUD ABU AL'WAFA (1910? - 1970?) Born in Egypt, he could not finish his education because of poverty. Lost a leg when young and always walked on crutches and wore a qalibayah (long shirt) to hide his wooden leg. Became a public servant in the Ministry of Education and wrote poems for schoolboys. He was influenced by the writings of the Sufi mystics.

AL-MUNSIF AL-WAHAYBI (1949 -) Born in Tunisia, he now teaches Arabic literature at high schools and writes modern poetry.

ABD AL-RAZAQ ABD AL-WAHID (1930 -) Born in Iraq and educated at the Teachers Training College in Baghdad. A pioneer of modern poetry, he has been a leading Iraqi poet for 30 years, writing classical and modern poetry which has been translated into several languages. Received the first Saddan Poetry Prize in Iraq in 1987.

KHALIFA AL-WUQAYYAN (1941 -) Born in Kuwait, attended Cairo University, and obtained PhD from Ain Shams University in 1980. Now an official of the National Council for Culture, Arts and Literature in Kuwait and has taken major part in its program of disseminating Arabic and world culture to a wide Arab audience. Has published 2 collections of classical poetry.

ISA AL-YASIRI (1942 -) Born in Amara, Iraq, he is a farmer and a prolific poet. He is a modernist who writes with great feeling for imagery. Has published 5 collections of verse.

SA'DI YUSUF (1943 -) Born in Basra, Iraq and graduated from Baghdad Teachers Training College in 1955. Taught at schools in Iraq, Algeria and Lebanon. Former member of the Iraqi Communist Party, he now lives in Cyprus. He is a modernist and has published 4 volumes of poetry.

MUHAMMAD MAHMUD AL-ZUBAIRI (1909 - 1964) Born in Sanaa in North Yemen; studied at religious schools and then at University of Cairo. Returned to yemen after the 1962 revolution and became Minister of Education and member of the Executive Council. Killed by royalist forces in 1964 and has since been regarded as one of Yemen's martyrs. Published several collections of classical poetry.

NOTE: Grateful thanks are due to Dr Hussam al-Khatibe, Professor Abdel Wahid Lulua, Dr Ali Shalash, Dr Nurradin Sammud, and the Australian embassies in London, Paris, Algeria, Syria, Jordan, Egypt and Saudi Arabia for their help in compiling these notes. Please advise the publishers of any errors so that these may be corrected in any future editions.

TRANSLITERATION OF NAMES

The names in the text and Notes have been transliterated from the Arabic according to traditional western style. The names listed here follow the modern international conventions. Thanks are due to Dr Samar Attar for her invaluable help with the task of transliteration.

Luṭfī Jaʿfar Amān
Lameʿa ʿAbbas ʿAmārah
Hilāl al-ʿĀmirī
Saʿīd Aql
Ḥasan Fath al-Bāb
S̲h̲awqī Bag̲h̲dādī
Ḥamrī Baḥrī
ʿAbdullāh al-Baradūnī
ʿAbd al-Wahab al-Bayātī
Babhā Bin Bedāywah
Maḥmūd Darwīsh
Amal Dunqal
Muḥammad Ḥasan Faqī
Muhammad al-Fāyiz
ʿAbdullah al-Fayṣal
Muḥammad al-Faytūrī
Muḥammad Abduh G̲h̲ānim
Muḥammad al-G̲h̲azzi
Qāsim Ḥaddād
Buland al-Ḥaidarī
Sārah Ḥārib
Muḥammad al-Ḥārīthī
Ẓāfir al-Ḥasan

K̲h̲alīl Ḥāwī
Aḥmad ʿAbd al-Muʿṭī Ḥijāzī
Muḥammad al-Makkī Ibrāhīm
Samāʾ Īsā
Badawī al-Jabbal
Muḥammad Mahdī al-Jawāhirī
Salma al-K̲h̲aḍrā al-Jayyūsī
Īlyās K̲h̲alīl Juryis
Yūsuf al-K̲h̲al
Bis̲h̲ārah al-K̲h̲ūrī
Ṣalaḥ Labakī
Ḥasan al-Lawzī
Īlīyā Abū Māḍī
ʿAlī Mīrzā Maḥmūd
Ḥaydar Maḥmūd
Aḥmad al-Majātī
Jaʿfar Mājid
Nāzik al-Mālaʾikah
S̲h̲afīq al-Maʿlūf
Abd al-Azız al-Maqaliḥ
Aḥmad Maṭar
Aḥmad al-Ṣāfī al-Najafī
Ibrāhīm Nājī

Ibrāhīm Naṣrallah
ʿĪsā al-Naʿūrī
Nizār Qabbānī
Samīḥ al-Qāsim
Ḥasan ʿAbdullāh al-Qurashī
Ghāzī al-Quṣaibī
ʿAbd al-Raḥmān Rafīʿ
Geelī ʿAbd al-Raḥmān
ʿAbd al-Munʿim al-Rifāʿi
ʿUmar Abū Rīshah
Adīb Saʿb
ʿAli al-Sabʿtī
Ṣalāḥ Abd al-Ṣabūr
ʿAlī Aḥmad Saʿīd
Muḥammad al-Akhḍar al-Sāʿiḥī
Aḥmad Ṣālih al-Ṣālih
Ruʾā Sālim
Nūrradīn Ṣammūd
Muḥammad al-Sarghīnī
George Ṣaydaḥ
Ḥabīb al-Ṣāyegh
Yūsuf al-Ṣāyegh
Badr Shākir al-Sayyāb
Īlyās Abū Shabakah
Aḥmad al-Shārif
ʿAlī al-Sharqāwī
Muḥammad Ibrāhīm Abū Ṣinnah
Ḥusain Sirḥān

ʿAbd al-Karīm al-Ṭabbāl
Mubārak Bin Saif Al Thānī
Fadwā Ṭūqān
Azrāj ʿUmar
Ibrāhīm al-Usṭā Umar
Muḥammad ʿUmrān
Ibrāhīm al-Urayyiḍ
Thurayyā al-Urayyiḍ
Maḥmud Abu al-Wāfa
Al-Munsif al-Waḥaybī
ʿAbd al-Razāq ʿAbd al-Wāḥid
Khalīfa al-Wuqayyān
ʿĪsā al-Yāsirī
Saʿdī Yūsuf
Muḥammad Maḥmūd al-Zubairī

Other publications of The Leros Press:

CENTURY OF CLOUDS by Geoff Page and Wendy Coutts
Translations from the French of Guillaume Apollinaire

MIRACLES OF DISBELIEF by Andrew Taylor and Beate Josephi
Translations from the German of Christine Lavant, Ingeborg Bachmann, Sarah Kirsch and Ursula Krechel

ROAD TO THE MOUNTAINS by Reginald de Bray
Translations from the Macedonian of Radovan Pavlovski

THE SCULPTOR OF CANDLES by J.R.Rowland
An anthology of Voznesensky and other contemporary Russian poets

THE POET'S LAMP by Alfred French
An anthology of Czech poetry

With Prosveta Press of Belgrade
POEMS FROM NORWAY Reginald de Bray's translation of the Serbian poems of Desanka Maksimovic

THE EARTH IS HOLLOW by the brilliant Greek-Australian writer Dimitris Tzoumacas. Original text with translations by Dina Tourva and Fotini Sidiropoulos